The Modern Soccer Coach: Pre-Season Training

by Gary Curneen

BENNION KEARNY

Published by Bennion Kearny Limited
6 Woodside
Churnet View Road
Oakamoor
Staffordshire
ST10 3AE

www.BennionKearny.com

Inside images (as marked): ©Academy Soccer Coach

To Erin, Calum, and Roy.

My inspiration every day.

About the Author

Gary Curneen is the Head Women's Soccer Coach at California State University Bakersfield. Gary holds a UEFA 'A' License from the Irish FA and a "Premier Diploma" from the NSCAA. Gary also gained a Master's in Business Administration from Wingate University, where he coached the Lady Bulldogs to a 95-48-8 record along with their first ever SAC Championship and place in the NCAA Tournament. In 2013 he worked as the Assistant Coach at University of Cincinnati.

Gary has played and coached at the collegiate level in the United States for more than ten years. His coaching education has seen him travel to study the best teams in the world and how they work first hand. A lifelong learner, Gary is a player-centered coach who focuses on professionalism, responsibility, and accountability within the framework of each team he works with. He believes that creating a culture of excellence is paramount to success and that each training session should include physical, tactical, technical, and mental components that challenge the players to perform at a high level.

Gary is the author of the acclaimed best-selling coaching books: *The Modern Soccer Coach 2014: A Four Dimensional Approach* and *The Modern Soccer Coach: Position-Specific Training*

Acknowledgements

Thank you to my wife Erin. I could not have picked a more challenging time to write this book and you have supported me every step of the way. You are my strength and the best wife, mother, and best friend I could ever wish for. I love you with all of my heart.

I am blessed to have an incredible support system at home in Omagh, Northern Ireland, and in North Carolina that have helped so much in recent times. To all my family and friends; in particular, my parents Sean and Marian, sister Angie, brother-in-law Luke, mother-in-law Janice, thank you so much for being there. I love you all.

I would also like to thank my Publisher at Bennion Kearny, James Lumsden-Cook, for his expertise, patience and indispensable work throughout this process. Your advice, ability, and support have been invaluable throughout the writing of this book and it would not have been possible without your help.

A special thanks to the many coaches who have influenced my work in this book. Coaches like Tony Strudwick, David Tenney, Nathan Winder, Garga Caserta, Michael Watts, Danny Worthington, Clifton Bush, Michael Beale, Nate Lie, Neil Adair, Gary Hamill, Jeremy Hurdle, Tim Palmer, Richie Grant, Marty Gormley, Jed Davies, Alex Shultz, Gerald Boyle, Ian Barker, Sam Bensley, Neil Stafford, Gerry Cleary, and Ben Bartlett, have played a major role in my research and writing. I admire you all as professionals, but most importantly as people. In addition, thank you also to Academy Soccer Coach for their software and help with the tactical diagrams.

Academy Soccer Coach

Academy Soccer Coach is a company that provides digital solutions for coaches at every level of the game. Our coaching software enables coaches, clubs and professional organizations to plan and prepare their sessions remotely from anywhere in the world.

Academy Soccer Coach works with following the professional clubs and organizations:

Fulham FC, West Ham United FC, Stoke FC, Newcastle United FC, Crystal Palace FC, Portland Timbers Sporting Kansas City, National Soccer Coaches Association of America, US Soccer (Women's), The Irish

Football Association, The Professional Footballers Association, and many more.

For more information on Academy Soccer Coach and the services we provide please visit www.academysoccercoach.com

Illustrations (download)

If you are reading an electronic version of this book, you may find some of the illustrations difficult to explore fully on your Kindle or Nook or iPhone. Likewise, if you are reading the print version of the book and would like to get your hands on the illustrations anyway – we can help.

All the illustrations in this book are available as a freely downloadable color PDF.

Download the file from the publisher's website at: www.bennionkearny.com/gc501.pdf

Table of Contents

Chapter 5 - Games-Based Training   59

Chapter 6 - Sustaining High Intensity   77

1

Pre-Season Introduction

It is without doubt the most highly anticipated time of the year for any coach, regardless of the level at which they work. They have counted down the days on the calendar and played out every tactical scenario possible in their heads. The physical and mental battle scars of last season have been left on an exotic beach weeks ago, and everyone arrives to pre-season fresh and ready to go. Every player tends to start on a clean slate and, for a period of time, their shortcomings are put to the back of everyone's mind. The mind of a coach contains only positive images of what their players can do, rather than what they can't.

If there has been a summer tournament on TV, the majority of coaches will be arriving back with whatever tactical system has been trending on their brain, keen to try it with their own set of players. Although the media portray the opening day of the season as the day upon which hopes and dreams are born, the reality is that it starts much earlier for coaches. The new gear and equipment has arrived and ambitions are always set high. In addition, the staff always look forward to the social interaction with players: catching up on summer stories and reconnecting with friends at the club. There may even be one or two new faces to join the squad which adds a new dimension to team chemistry. It is a period of time when potential and dreams dominate. There really is nothing quite like pre-season for a coach.

The irony is, however, that the players have always taken a different view – almost the exact opposite in fact. For a player, pre-season typically means running, brutal physical work, more running, sore legs, even more running, and then plenty of blisters. Say the word 'pre-season' to any player at any level, of any generation, and you will be met with exasperated looks and plenty of similar responses. The majority of players hate it and if there was a stronger word than hate, I would use it. Whereas coaches see the rewards of hard work, the majority of players see punishment. Even in the modern game, with periodization charts and state-of-the-art recovery systems in place, the response from players remains the same. When Manchester City kicked off their training in the summer of 2015, midfielder Yaya Toure was asked if he was excited to be back with the team. "Pre-season is not something I like at all," he replied – and the majority of players around the world nodded in agreement.

Evolution of pre-season

If you look at what previous generations went through in pre-season, you can almost sympathize with many players' universal distain of it. Up until the 1990s, pre-season was primarily about survival. It was seen as a necessary evil that players had to go through, in order to play the game they loved.

Even at the highest levels, summer breaks for players were all about catching up on junk food and alcohol, without the scrutiny or constant input from coaches. As the same players reported in for pre-season camp, they did so resigned to the fact that they had to shed the pounds fast and it was going to be miserable. They were accepting of their punishment. In some cases, bin bags were even given out before sessions to help sweat more of the unwanted weight away quicker.

Another traditional aspect of pre-season camps was the bonding created as a result of the endless runs over mountains, sand, and roads. Teams that suffered together, seemingly grew stronger. Misery loves company and there was no better example of that than a pre-season locker room. Moans and groans united the players and got them through the long and painful days.

From a coaching level, pre-season was very much an authoritarian model. Players were told what to do and they did it. Nothing was recorded and session plans would be mistaken for a Crossfit program today. Some coaches even handed their teams over to army fitness staff who gave them two or three days of regimented work before they were taken back to their training headquarters exhausted and thankful of the glorious day when footballs actually came out.

Of course, the game today has evolved and changed. Not only are the financial rewards higher than ever before with the game now under a global spotlight, but it is played in a much more different way than any other era in the history of the game. Below are just some of the current trends of the modern era:

Intensity and Speed – The pace of the game has increased largely because of two reasons. Today's athletes are bigger, faster, and stronger so can produce more power and cover ground quicker. Secondly, technical skills training starts at a younger age so players are more equipped technically to deal with the ball and play at speed.

Emphasis on Tactical Awareness – Teams today are better organized defensively and players today have a higher tactical understanding because of their exposure to a variety of systems early in their development. Tactical conversations are now part of every highlights show in every country with almost every coaching decision discussed in detail by today's 'experts'.

Possession Based Teams – Retention of the ball is no longer a luxury afforded to the best teams. The majority of teams today are comfortable in possession of the ball and have a number of players who can hurt the opposition with time and space. The technical skills required to play the game have risen significantly.

Different Personalities – Society has dramatically changed the makeup of teams. A coach today has to manage a wide range of personalities, along with players from different backgrounds and cultures.

Impact of Technology – Social media has had a huge impact on the level of scrutiny facing coaches at all levels. After a game, everyone from fans to parents to people with just a passing interest in the game take to the message boards and dissect a team's performance. With most of the criticism directed towards the coach of the losing team, almost all levels of the game have become results-driven to a certain extent.

Player Power – The dynamics of a locker room have changed due to the economic shift in the game over the past ten years. With increased salaries and marketing power, players are now more valuable than the coach. If player unrest rises along with poor results, it is almost certain that the coach will not survive.

So with all these changes, the big question that we must ask is this: have coaches adapted their pre-season work alongside changes in the modern game? If we look at some training programs with expensive monitoring systems, and a training pitch with enough cones to resemble an airport runway, you would be forgiven for thinking that it has. But if we actually look beyond the fancy technology and extravagant set-up, the reality is that many coaches have not adapted their pre-season program, nor do they intend to. Coaching may have seen something of a revolution in recent years, but pre-season seems to have been one of the last aspects of the game to catch up. It is still being delivered in largely the same way it always has been, and because of this, is viewed by all players in exactly the same way as Yaya Toure views it.

The Modern Soccer Coach

Asking coaches to change their methods and work may be easier said than done of course. Habits play a huge role in the reluctance of many to move forward or even question whether current practices are applicable to the game today. Many cling to a tried-and-tested model, even if its effectiveness can be seriously questioned. As coaches, we are almost preprogramed to prescribe the same type of physical training to our players that we were 'forced' to endure ourselves, for the simple reason that "that's just the way we have always done it." Too many fall into the trap of believing that simple hard work is enough. They hear the players moan and groan, and judge the difficulty of the session by the volume, rather than the quality of it. Coaches today grew up in a 'no pain, no gain' world and with it comes the temptation to teach our players the values that were delivered to ourselves as players. Of course, traditional values like hard work and the correct attitude will always be important factors of the game, but the reality is that if all our focus is simply centered around those areas, players and teams won't get better individually or collectively.

In a traditional pre-season set-up, the majority of the squad typically fall under at least one of the categories below:

Bored Players – Constant long distance running and conditioning sessions fail to engage or inspire players to work hard and many simply count down the time for the session to finish. You don't have to ask them, but simply observe body language and you can see they are there in body but not mind.

Injured Players – With only a certain amount of time to work with players before the first game arrives, many coaches heap huge physical and mental loads on their players during the first couple of days. Combined with the long duration of sessions, it is just a matter of time before players pick up injuries and rule them out of both training sessions and games.

Confused Players –If the players are overloaded physically, the opposite could be said about their technical training. When the balls eventually do come out, coaches are playing catch-up and do not have enough sessions to prepare their players for games.

Angry Players – With the team unprepared for the opening games, the season begins with poor results that cause a breakdown in the relationship between players and staff. The authoritarian approach from the coaches during pre-season continues with a divide now created between players and coaches.

Different approaches and different results

Jose Mourinho decided to try something different in July of 2015. Two months earlier, his Chelsea team won the Premier League by such a distance, that even a poor finish to their campaign had no effect on the title race. Looking back on his victorious season, Mourinho was concerned about the sluggish and tired finish towards the end and decided to adapt the pre-season program to combat this for the following season. The usual intensity and focus would now be built up over a period of time, instead of demanded from players from day one. Chelsea would ease their way into the season and peak at the right time when Champions League honors would be at stake. Mourinho made no attempt to hide this strategy in front of the media and after a shock defeat to New York Red Bulls, he played down the importance of the summer program. "Pre-season is fake, for good and for bad. If you're very bad it's fake, and if you're too good it's fake." Chelsea, however, took their poor run of performances into the new season and never recovered. Of course, as we all know by now, Jose Mourinho was sacked in December with Chelsea unbelievably losing nine of their first sixteen Premier League games, and sitting in 16th place of the Premier League.

At the same time, Arsene Wenger went in another direction and made a conscious decision to treat the 2015 pre-season with the upmost importance. His Arsenal team was going to mean business from day one and when he took them to Malaysia for the Barclays Asia Trophy, he assured fans that they would be taking every game seriously. Similar to Mourinho, Wenger shared his intentions with the worldwide media, "We had a good preparation and a good preparation brings confidence. It doesn't give you a guarantee that you start strong in the competition but it's still better for the confidence and the belief of the group. Then, when it comes down to points, you add that little bit of extra commitment that is demanded in games." After winning all of their pre-season games, Arsenal defeated Chelsea to win the Community Shield and won seven out of their first ten Premier League games. They built on that momentum, in all competitions and finished in second place in the Premier League, with many people believing they should have done even better.

Of course, a strong pre-season does not guarantee success but this season in the Premier League has shown that if you get it wrong, it can have dramatic effects on your team, both mentally and physically. We may not know exactly what specifically Chelsea or Arsenal did differently on the training ground, or how they managed their players physically, but we do know what kind of message was delivered to the players and how impactful that proved to be.

Even at the highest level, players must know that they are investing hard work in a purpose that will pay off. The game does not possess a neutral gear so telling players that games or training sessions don't count will always risk setting the team backwards. However, taking pre-season seriously is not about simply announcing how important it is or telling your players that it is tough. They must *feel* its importance in every single aspect of the program. Culture and environment are where successful teams thrive when it comes to transferring good intentions into great actions. Setting a winning mentality was exactly how Jose Mourinho set himself apart during his first period as Chelsea manager, when he announced to the world that they would aim to win every game in every competition. He then backed that up with extensive work on the training field, prepared detailed tactical dossiers on opponents, and placed a strong emphasis on positive relationships with every one of his players. Confidence and momentum are both critical factors when it comes to success in sport but they don't come easily and coaches cannot plan to pick them up midway through the season without setting the foundation at the beginning.

Changing the mindset

Let's look more closely at the impact of culture and compare the pre-season training environment of two different teams.

Team One arrives on the field 30 minutes before the session starts. Everyone is together and you can already feel the positive energy through the laughter and loud conversations. As players begin their preparation, you can sense an almost business-like approach descending over the group. Each player is fully aware of the physical and technical standards that they will be required to deliver once the session begins and when it does, the intensity is electric. There is a purpose behind every action on the field and the competition levels are sky high. Nobody wants to lose any game or exercise. When coaching points are made, players also offer each other feedback before implementing the improvements in the next set. After the session, players voluntarily request to stay for positional work and walk off the field in deep conversation with coaches and teammates. The dialogue continues in the team meeting and everyone has an input during the tactical discussions. The players are slow to leave as they spend their time in the training room with the medical staff, already preparing for another big day tomorrow.

Now let's take a visit to Team Two. Twenty minutes before the session starts, players begin to walk out onto the field, slowly in groups of twos and threes, dreading to even ask what the coach has set-up for them today. Half the squad is still in the medical room, where a group of injured players are joined by the weary and sore who seek refuge and only wait until the last possible minute to get out on the pitch. Complaints dominate almost every conversation, but the coaching staff cannot hear beneath the whispers. The session starts slowly as the players have yet to 'check-in' mentally. As a result, the tempo is low along with the quality of technical ability. As passes go wayward, frustration levels rise from both coaches and players. Coaching points are delivered to players who are too tired to understand, or who look as if they do not care to make the required changes. The threat of more physical work does lift the intensity of the session, but the quality never reaches the standard required. The session debrief from the coaching staff centers around attitude and application. "We need to work harder," the players are continually told by the coaching staff. It feels like a wasted session for the coaches as they walk off the field and return to the locker room only to find that the players have already gone home.

What team would you want to work with, or be associated with, especially with the season fast approaching? Obviously, the majority of us would choose Team One. The biggest difference between the two teams lies solely in the culture of the team and the attitude of the players. The first group wanted to be there, they wanted to work hard, they wanted to stay there, and they wanted to prepare to make tomorrow even better. The second group arrived with a negative mindset, were reluctant to train, were too exhausted to take on information, lacked the energy needed to drive the quality of the session, and could not wait to leave once they were dismissed. This is why the most important challenge for a coach arrives before the first pre-season session even starts. They must aim to break down the huge mental barrier that holds players back during arguably the most important period of the season. The hatred, anxiety, and negativity that seem to arise when you simply utter the word 'pre-season' have got to be removed.

Although Team One may seem slightly idealistic, if we know how important the role of culture and environment play in success, along with confidence and momentum, why are we not aiming to get it right from day one? Players who hate the training will not push themselves to excel but instead push themselves to get through it. Checking off training sessions may feel good at the time, but successful teams don't operate like that. For a team to reach anywhere near their potential, they must be operating at their maximum, physically, technically, tactically, and mentally, every single day. It must become second nature to push through training sessions in the same way you can push through the final minutes of a game and get the desired result.

Former Southampton and England player James Beattie believes that the key to a player's performance is in their mindset. "Sports science and fitness may make that 3-4% difference, but lose a player's mind and 50% of him may disappear." Following a periodization model designed for a professional team or standing with a whistle while you conduct Olympic-style testing may not necessarily be poor practice for a coach, but it may not work for your team. The coach must get the balance right. It must be challenging and tough, but also enjoyable and engaging. The coaches must set the standards, but it is up to the players to drive it. If coaching staff do get the balance right, however, it can be powerful enough to propel the team towards heights that they have never reached before. There is nothing more powerful than players who embrace a culture of hard work and who have a collective desire to both improve and achieve. It turns the doubters into believers, and more importantly, turns close games into big victories.

Goal of this book

The goal of this book is certainly not to argue against hard work being the fundamental currency of a successful pre-season program. Of course, a work ethic is required and we can never overlook the power of attitude if we want to set ourselves up for a great season. The players must know that they are investing work that will subsequently pay off throughout the season so the work must be challenging and difficult. Tough training sessions ultimately create tough teams.

We will also not eliminate the running aspect of the game as high intensity runs are a critical component of performance. Instead, we will look at how to effectively plan and implement a program that will prepare the players for the rigors of top level competition and optimize their performance, both individually and collectively. Hard work must be accompanied by quality if you are to be successful in the game today. In addition, if we can get our players to commit to our work like never before and go above and beyond in other areas, then our chances of success increase dramatically. Below are the ways in which we shall aim to do that:

1. Remove the negative stereotypes associated with pre-season training. Instead of players thinking punishment, we want them to think rewards. Winners love putting the work in.

2. Increase the awareness of our players so they understand the system of play. All training will be relevant to how we will play.

3. Redefine match fitness, and specifically what we need, from our players on the physical side of the game. Establishing what physical factors will be important for how we want to play, and then training those throughout the season.

4. Improve team and individual performance through a training program which focuses on key moments that players will find themselves in throughout the season.

5. Develop a support system around training that creates a 'buy-in' from players who want to commit to the process rather than comply. We will look at how to impact diet so that they can recover quickly from sessions and establish important habits that will help them remain healthy throughout the season.

6. Build team spirit. Establish a winning culture that is co-owned by both players and staff alongside a competitive environment where players enjoy training and want to work hard for the team, staff, and themselves.

Let's get started!

2

Before You Start...

There can be many different interpretations about what qualifies as a successful pre-season, but if the goal of the coaching staff is simply to 'work the players hard' and 'get them fit', there is no way they are preparing their team to achieve anywhere near its potential.

It is somewhat ironic that the same coaches who spend so much time worrying about players reporting into pre-season unfit, complain about their condition when they do arrive, and announce after the first defeat that they aren't fit enough. These are the same coaches who make the pre-season program up as they go along and judge the sessions by miles logged or misery inflicted, regardless of intensity, focus, or quality. It is a widespread problem in the game today. Too many coaches are taking short cuts and planning in their heads – which is great if they can do it – but as the team grows and the games arrive, the team must know who they are, where they are going, and how the coaching staff intends for them to get there.

The first step for coaches to change how we think, prepare, and present pre-season to our team is to actually take responsibility for it. The coach and his/her staff must structure the work, choose the correct exercises, manage the load, set the tone in terms of intensity, and lead by example with their energy and enthusiasm. Of course it's not easy but if we cannot get that right, we can forget about a winning culture, shared ownership, and 'buy-in' from players.

Coaches are in the driving seat at the beginning of pre-season and must remain so throughout. Those who let players dictate the route, do so at their peril.

The second step to maximizing our time in pre-season is to remove all generalizations associated with our program and instead be as specific as possible about both what we want to achieve and how we are going to measure it. If coaches are continually talking about working hard and effort, the players and teams are not getting tactically better by solving problems and dealing with scenarios that will present themselves in the upcoming games. So our coaching points must move beyond work and effort, if we want to improve as a team.

As we will see in this book, there is so much more to pre-season than running. Every team gets around 3-6 weeks in pre-season so there is always enough time where we can make up ground in physical preparation but if players are not confident in the game plan and their ability to execute it when under pressure, they will always fall short sooner rather than later. We must always keep in mind that 'The best way to predict the future is to create it'.

Establish a Model of Play

Before we even start to focus on the fitness and physical aspects of pre-season, the coach must develop a model of play, which the team will adopt throughout the season. This part of planning is perhaps the most critical step in pre-season because it will define exactly what match fitness is and how we need to prepare our players on every level (physical, technical, tactical, and mental).

You cannot talk about match fitness before deciding how you want the actual match to look.

A playing model is similar to a coaching philosophy but is slightly more practical and goes into a little more depth, identifying crucial areas and taking a number of factors into consideration which can impact philosophy. The primary purpose of a playing model is to define exactly what the team intends to become over a period of time. It is neither a set of formations or tactics, but instead contains detailed principles that the team will adopt throughout their training and games. Barcelona coach, Luis Enrique, believes in the basics when it comes to identifying the playing model: "It's the coach's job to decide his team's style of play, how they attack and how they defend. They have to be effective at both ends of the pitch." Without a plan or model, the team is essentially rudderless, handing over responsibility to luck and excuses.

Playing Model Examples

Playing models can be constructed in a number of different ways and are not exclusively designed for elite and senior level where results and pressure reign. They can also be used at the youth level where part of the emphasis is on coaching and developing both the team and the individual player. The model below is designed by youth coach, Sam Bensley, who focuses on the development side of coaching. In Sam's model, he

The Modern Soccer Coach

identifies the individual goals for each player he has, alongside his tactical model. For youth coaches this is very important because, in essence, you are still teaching the game. The playing model here defines the basics but also educates players on how to learn systems and critical areas that they will see more of as they develop and get older. Too often, development is regarded as skill and technical qualities, but more and more players are arriving at a higher level without an understanding of the game. By separating the team and the player, Sam allows young players to become more process-orientated and patient in their development. It is a crucial tool to communicate key growth areas with parents and club coaches.

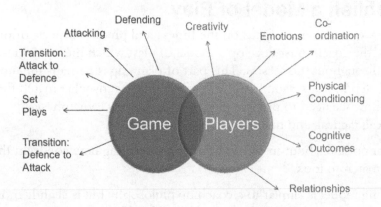

The second example of a playing model is designed by Tim Palmer, who coaches at St Joseph's College in Australia and who also works as an analyst for Prozone. Tim works with older players who are now at the stage where results are part of the criteria. He has highlighted similar themes to Sam but has added sub-sections within each area that he also focuses on. As a result, his model is slightly more complex with additional information, both in and out of possession, for his players to interpret and understand. Without having seen his team play, we can tell from his language and terminology that he wants his team to control the game through possession and press high and compactly as a unit. Tim is dealing with older players so the terminology can become a little bit more complex, as can the tactical ideas.

Game Model - St Josephs College 2016

Key Principles

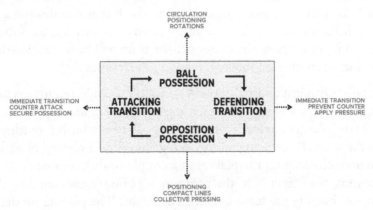

Once the playing model is established, the primary goal of the coaching staff is now to communicate it effectively to the players. This is such an important process because it clarifies purpose and direction and allows everyone to see the aims and objectives of your system. It tells everyone where you are going, and gives you a map. It also acts as a foundation through which all training and conversations on the field should be derived. Below are a number of reasons why a playing model is important to have before the pre-season period starts.

Flexibility – A playing model is much stronger than a formation, primarily because of its flexibility. A coach can still apply the same principles from the playing model but use a different formation. The best example of this is Pep Guardiola, who has used dozens of formations at Bayern Munich during his three years there but his principles have remained consistent. While a playing model can be set and consistent, formations can also change, based on the opponent or the score. A formation is not a strong enough foundation from which to build.

Removes Panic – If results don't go your way when the games start up, the last thing you want to be doing as a coach is questioning fitness levels, team selection, refereeing decisions, or all three of the above. With an effective playing model established, coaches can see what is not working or what needs improvement and then prioritize their work. It allows coaches to remain calm while they plan their work and then work their plan.

Enhances Communication – Nothing frustrates players more than mixed messages from the coaching staff which results in confusion over assumed roles and responsibilities. The playing model gives the players and coaching staff a common ground from which they can discuss a variety of different themes. The more soccer-based conversations that can happen within a program, the better off the team will be as relationships are built and strengthened through regular interactions.

Set Specific Objectives For Players – Good coaching requires setting specific goals and standards, and then managing them throughout the season. Many players have one pre-season goal: to establish a starting place in the team. By creating and working alongside a playing model, the staff are now challenging the players in a couple of different ways. It's not about beating out Player X to the position, it's about understanding the position and helping the team become successful. The playing model is also designed to enhance the quality and quantity of feedback.

Gives Team Purpose and Direction – To be successful in the long-term, a team requires an identity beyond simply trying to win games. The stronger the identity, the more the players are willing to put into the team, both on and off the field. Focusing frantically on what matters most, daily, energizes a team and energy is gold dust during pre-season and beyond.

Empowers The Players – The best way to maximize players' energy and focus levels, is to give them co-ownership of their journey. Once players have a responsibility to the team, great things begin to happen and they will commit even more energy and commitment to the cause. Accountability soon becomes second nature and no player wants to let down their team.

Influence Planning Of Training Content – Once the playing model is established, it will drive the session planning and make it much easier to prioritize work. In the book *Pep Confidential*, Guardiola's assistant coach, Lorenzo Buenaventura commented on the consistency between Guardiola's model and his training methodology. "Each exercise incorporates an aspect of Pep's football philosophy."

How To Develop A Model Of Play

It takes time to develop a model and a number of factors must be taken into consideration. Below are seven ways that it can be built and developed by the coaching staff.

1. **Identify the strengths of your team** – The model should be built with the players in mind. That must be the starting point.

The players should be evaluated on every level (technical, physical, tactical, and mental) before deciding on what areas to prioritize.

2. **Stick To Your Beliefs** – A playing model must also be consistent with the principles of the game which the coach values most highly. These can change from coach to coach and can be somewhat unique. The beautiful thing about the game is that we all interpret it in a slightly different way so this is the coach's opportunity to put their own spin on their work.

3. **Create a Common Language** – Although the team can all speak the same language, the coach can sometimes use a dialogue which the players do not understand. All staff and players should be aware and use the same terminology and understand the correct context in which it is used.

4. **Keep It Simple** – The idea is not to confuse the players, nor highlight the knowledge of the coach. The more complex your views on the game are, the more you should break them into pieces for the players so they can digest the information more easily. Simple is harder than complex and successful coaches are very good at breaking the game down to help players understand information and apply it to their game.

5. **Be Realistic** – We all want to play like Barcelona but the reality is that most of us are not fortunate to play at the Nou Camp every other week. Your playing model instead must be consistent with the playing styles and abilities of your players. When developing his own model, Jose Mourinho said: "You can't create a contradiction with the idea you want for the game. If your team does not play from the back in a game, do not incorporate this in your exercises."

6. **Share It** – We have already mentioned that the playing model must be clear in the minds of the coaching staff; let's not forget that the players are the most important recipients of it. If they consistently hear messages relating back to it, the chances of them embracing it increases. When players are mindful of the process that drives results, teams begin to intentionally improve.

7. **Stick With It** – Having a playing model does not guarantee success but working hard at it over a long period of time does give you a great opportunity. Even after a defeat, it is important that the coaching staff review and understand that this is a process and that things grow through time, and most importantly, quality work. It's not enough for players to understand a system of play.

They must buy into it, and have belief that they can master it and perform it under pressure.

Develop Match Fitness

Once we have clearly defined how we want our team to play, the next step is to prepare them physically to perform these functions and roles continuously for 90 minutes.

Traditional pre-season thinking leads us to believe that any form of continual training will naturally move general fitness levels of players to match fitness levels. However, Michael Watts, a Strength and Conditioning Coach who has worked in the Premier League for over eight seasons, believes that match and general fitness are mutually exclusive. "In my opinion match fitness comes from playing matches. Pre-season is the opportunity to prepare players in a progressive manner to increase volume and intensity through periodization which will focus on metabolic demands and strength gains."

Watts also points out that the more specific coaches can be, in terms of physical demands, the better the response from a player. "Most players now have a good general base fitness, the areas that need to be developed are usually the high-end demands such as, sprinting, high speed running, accelerations and decelerations."

This is consistent with how the game is changing on the physical side as players' total running distances have decreased while high-speed running is on the increase. The highest level is now about intensity rather than endurance.

Again, the coach has a responsibility to identify the specific physical requirements of the playing model, and then adapt the exercises and training sessions to develop those attributes within the player. For example, if you want to press high up the field, not only must the attacking players become conditioned to sustain high levels of work, but the defenders must work on playing a high line, too, and become comfortable with space in behind them. The staff must therefore identify what the physical demands look like for a player and only then can sessions be designed to mirror the demands of the game. Watts believes that once the playing model is established, the training must be consistent for results to occur – and it takes time: "I think a player needs at least 4 weeks to adapt to a style of play and we have seen this in our objective GPS data when a new manager comes to a club during the season."

If the coach is fortunate enough to have access to a Strength and Conditioning coach or a Sports Science Department, it is crucial that they are on the same page. The volume of work in a pre-season program can be pretty heavy on even the fittest of players but coaches will always complain that there is not enough time, so will naturally want to train more and more. A modern coach must be open to input from experts in this field, who can advise on fatigue symptoms and recovery strategies that can help them keep their players strong and healthy.

Create a Winning Culture

In Chapter 1, we briefly discussed the role which culture and environment plays in the success of a team. It is the foundation from which winning teams are built and has a direct effect on results throughout the season. Quite simply, culture drives behaviour, behaviour drives habits, and habits inevitably create the performance.

So let's look closer at how you establish that culture during the pre-season period; the more things we can get our players to do right *off the pitch*, the more we can get them to do right on it.

The first thing we must recognize is that culture is never accidental. The coach is always responsible for it and, if shaped the wrong way, it is a very difficult thing to get back on track. It is also a great recruiting tool as the best players always want to work with the best and go where standards are high and demanding. Below are a number of ways in which the culture can be built and developed.

Establish Set of Standards – The players must be aware of what is expected in every aspect of the program. What will be tolerated and what will not. The more inexperienced the team is, the more specific these standards need to be. It is less about rules and more about educating your players as to why things have to be done a certain way. Building a culture is more about subtraction than addition. You must get rid of comfort zones and negativity before you can add anything.

Outline Individual Commitment Levels – Once you identify the standards required, you now need players to commit to them rather than simply comply. This is the most time-consuming task of culture management, but important nonetheless. Nothing demotivates committed players more than surrounding them with uncommitted players.

Set A Leadership Structure – Although the coaching staff are responsible for creating the culture, they cannot spend all of their time policing it or the players will never 'buy-in'. How standards are lived when the coaches are not around is sometimes the best way to assess culture. Therefore, the team needs a core group of players who both live and breathe it, and have a voice on the team. When I began coaching, an experienced coach once told me, "Your team will only be as good as your senior players." If the staff are lucky, this leadership group may come naturally. If not, it will have to be developed through time and work – but you cannot create co-ownership without it.

No Excuses – There will rarely be perfect conditions in which to perform throughout the season. Tough moments, bad pitches, and refereeing decisions happen to every team, but they cannot be used as a crutch for poor performances. Building a winning culture is therefore all about replacing excuse makers with problem solvers. Body language should be watched closely during pre-season and players should always be made aware if they show any negativity around the team. Tough always beats tired and that message should be sent to the players from day one.

Fight for It – The easiest part is setting the culture, the difficult part is keeping standards high. It takes enormous energy to maintain a culture as coaches must look and listen for behavior that they necessarily don't want to see or hear. It is natural that players will push boundaries every single day so you must be prepared to confront and deal with destructive behaviors before they embed themselves in the team culture. If you ignore it, you condone it.

Responsibilities of Coaching Staff

If we expect our players to commit to a high level of standards and values throughout the season, as coaches, we should not be exempt from the same. Your staff must be a collective group if you want to maximize your pre-season training and start the season the right way.

Enthusiasm – A low energy coach cannot expect to create a high energy environment. Diego Simeone at Atletico Madrid is a coach who drives his culture by the philosophy of, "I try to live each day like it's the last, with enthusiasm and ideas which I communicate to my players. Football is my life." Passion can attract and keep the attention of many players, so a coach must make sure they arrive to practice energized and ready to inspire the players and staff every day,

Lead By Example – I strongly believe that a coach should be a strong example of the culture that they are attempting to promote. If this means creating a physically fit team with a strong work ethic, then yes, the coach should also be physically fit. If communication is at the centre of team culture, the coach must always engage in conversation with players and should not be on their phone all the time. Little things make a big difference and a coach should never let the strength of the culture be questioned because they talk it but refuse to walk it.

Make It Safe – Part of the responsibility of staff should be to keep players healthy by managing their training loads and volume of work. If there is no sports science expert on staff, then education must be part of the off-season agenda. Coaches must seek both information and innovative ways to improve performance. The game is changing very quickly and it's easier than ever to get left behind.

Make it Challenging – As players improve and become better, the challenge point must also rise so that difficulty levels enable teams to keep pushing. The same training over time will produce the same results. For the session planning, balance is really important. Repetition is needed to improve and master skills, but creativity from coaches is required to facilitate the learning also.

Be Consistent – The staff should be a 'panic free zone' throughout pre-season and leading into the season. Michael Watts, referenced above, believes that a weakness of pre-season planning is that a bad result or gut feelings drive needless changes without enough review about what has been done in the past.

Be Appreciative – If you want your players to continue to go above and beyond in terms of work rate and commitment, you must continually acknowledge it. What gets recognized tends to get repeated and if players feel that there is 'no pleasing the coach', they will eventually drop their standards.

Be Personable – Exceptional coaches understand that inspiring and connecting with their players is much more powerful than controlling them. The values and actions of a coach are a lot more powerful in shaping team culture than a set of rules.

Conclusion

Most teams have potential entering pre-season, but only a select few realize it, develop it, and go on to become successful at the end of the season. Even at the highest level with Leicester City in the Premier League this year, you can see the 'difference makers'; they exude focused effort, total commitment, and a collective drive to both work hard and achieve. These elements are just as important, if not more so, than ability and talent.

How many teams work hard during pre-season? Almost all by their own assessment. How many teams work smart during pre-season? Not enough of them in my opinion. Arsene Wenger believes the coach must set the tone before pre-season even starts, "A preparation that is not serious does not give you any hope." The quality of planning and the definition of team style and execution are key for coaches and only after those are established can we focus on the delivery.

But the work is still only in its infancy. As long as coaches operate in an authoritarian control mode, the players will – at best – comply or become dependent on the coach.

As I mentioned in Chapter 1, creating training conditions was easier in past generations where coaching was simply about dictating information to players, and then standing back while they executed it. Coaching has become more complex now, and players today are given information through a multitude of mediums: in locker rooms, meeting rooms, 1v1 office talks, on their phones, and on iPads. As such, we must now create a model which empowers our players and inspires them to go above and beyond for the team.

Once players buy-in to the process and embrace the culture, you are on the way to maximizing potential. Mauricio Pochettino has developed a similar playing model at Tottenham to the one he created at Southampton and, more importantly, has also convinced his players to embrace an unbelievably high workload. Forward Harry Kane believes that this has been a driving force in their challenge for the title in 2016. "In pre-season there were double sessions, times when you were pushing yourself to the limit, but you're doing it for a reason. This is the reason that you're seeing now. As the season has gone on we've got fitter and fitter. I feel the fittest I've ever felt and the best shape I've ever been in. The gaffer did a lot of work in getting us fit."

Environments and culture do more to shape a team's mind-set and long term success than any other element. Once the foundation is set, the team is primed for intense and competitive sessions. Our next step is to look at the exercises which can now be delivered on the field to complement the culture set off it.

3

Counter Attacking

Counter attacking has exploded throughout the coaching world over the past five years. UEFA's study of the 2014/15 Champions League found that 20.6 per cent of goals came from teams using the fast break, but we have also seen it rise at amateur and youth levels.

It used to be seen as a negative way of playing, where teams "parked the bus" and tried to "nick one on the break", but it has now evolved into a destructive weapon that all successful teams seem to have at their disposal.

One ironic reason for the surge of counters is because of the defensive domination of opposition teams, rather than the defensive mentality of the counter attacking team. More and more teams are set up with a solid back four and two holding midfielders, so one of the most effective ways of breaking them down is to invite them into your half and take advantage when they are in possession of the ball.

Space is at a premium in the game today and it can really open up when a team has the ball, as they are advanced and dispersed; you will typically find both center backs split, full backs pushed up into attacking areas, and central midfielders rotating in order to create space by which to get on the ball. When you win possession in your half of the pitch, you have a matter of seconds to take advantage of the transition, and if you get it right it can be simply devastating. Leicester City is a perfect example of this in the 2015/16 Premier League and have thrown the possession statistics right out of the window with their ability to sit back, invite pressure, and then punish teams on the break.

Pre-season is a great time to work on counter attacking for a number of reasons. Physically, effective practice is extremely demanding on players and tests them to work at maximum speed over long distances. Technically it challenges both sides of the ball; attackers must dribble, combine, and finish on goal at full speed, while defenders will find themselves running back towards their own goal in game-like conditions.

Tactically, it is all about exposing teams who have lost their shape. Mentally, it works on decision making and creates many situations where players have to think fast. Overall, the focus is about taking advantage of space so every position, with and without the ball, has to work very hard to either capitalize on it, or recover from it.

Requirements for Counter Attacking

The best counter attacking teams are organized, understand their individual roles, and, most importantly, work very hard at it. A team is not naturally afforded the luxury simply because it possesses speed in attacking areas. There are many more variables to take into consideration, both in and out of possession. It is a style of play primarily about relationships between teammates, decisions made at full speed, and technical efficiency in key areas. Quality rather than quantity is definitely the name of the game, with the best teams sometimes only countering three times a game but able to score one or two goals from them. Here are some of the main points to take into consideration when looking at counter attacking with your team.

Defensive Strategy – Knowing how, and in what areas, you are looking to win the ball must be the first aspect of coaching counter attacking. If your team players are unclear of their defensive shape, you may win the ball back only to give it away again – and then *your* team is the one susceptible in transition. Teams at the highest level today are well organized, disciplined, and furthermore, are now setting traps for teams who are in possession, luring them into desired areas, and then pouncing on them. Again, looking at Leicester City as an example, they may have finished bottom of the pass completion chart in the Premier League, but they led the league in defensive interceptions and came third in tackles – both of which became the springboard for many successful counters.

Defensive Commitment – For counter attacking to work effectively with your team, you not only need a defensive strategy but you need the whole team to commit themselves 100% to it. A team cannot expect to break quickly with any forward who is unwilling to work… for two reasons. Firstly, the forward will not help them apply pressure and it only takes one player to switch off for teams to advance further up the pitch. Secondly, once the ball is regained, the same forward will always be on the back foot and not in the correct position for his teammates to play into. The best examples of this are Dimitar Berbatov and Mario Balotelli, who both struggled at Manchester United and Liverpool respectively in recent years, after both teams were excellent on the break prior to their arrivals.

Decision Makers – It is physically impossible to counter attack every time you win possession of the ball, so you need a group of players who can make the correct decision once they regain the ball. If the opposition are organized and compact when they lose the ball, the best option for your team will be to circulate the ball and look to build an attack through possession. However, if the opposition are out of balance, that is a good time to exploit matters and launch the counter. The decision to have a fast transition or controlled possession must be made in a matter of seconds so this is not something a coach can directly influence on the touchline.

Speed in Key Areas – There is no doubt that speed is *the* most important component of counter attacking. The more your team has of it, the more threats there are to the opposition. If you can get multiple options when you break, it can be almost impossible to defend against. Remember Carlo Ancelotti's Real Madrid in 2014 who countered with Ronaldo, Bale, Di Maria, and Benzema? Defensively, teams could not deal with them because the opposition could never get numbers back to provide cover and Real Madrid simply overran their opponents.

Numerical advantage – In the same way that you require players to commit themselves defensively to this system, they will also need to sprint long distances at their maximum to support the attack. Simply offering an option behind the ball is not enough, as attackers must have a willingness to run ahead of the ball in order to add depth to the attack, force defenders into areas that they do not wish to go, and create isolations. If you have multiple players who are willing to do this, you should create more overloads and have a greater opportunity of providing fluidity of movement in the attack. Both are nightmarish for defenders and will help your team score more goals.

Coaching the Counter

Because counter attacking requires speed of movement and quick thinking, coaches must be aware of how they teach and communicate its principles to their players. If you continually 'freeze' exercises and ask for explanations as to why a player chose one option or another, you may end up doing more harm than good. Coaches must be careful of creating 'paralysis by analysis', where players slow down to reassess decisions and lose the opportunity to take the initiative. Players sometimes only have seconds to make a decision so they must be aggressive with their decision making. You want them to take risks and try to play forward quickly, so second guessing will hinder that by slowing them down.

The Modern Soccer Coach

Another important aspect that you never want to take away as a coach is creativity. Attacking players need license to try things without fear of ramifications from their coach. Daniel Worthington, Head Coach of Canada's U-20 team, believes that triggers, rather than coaching points, are the key. He has broken counter attacking into 4 target areas or non-negotiables, and then allows the players the space and freedom to work within them.

1. **Win The Ball** – Getting your team to have an attacking mentality when defending is crucial to winning the ball in good areas. Dropping and shifting defensively can take you further from goal and make it harder to transition on the counter attack. There must be a certain area of the field where the team steps up their aggression levels in their pursuit of the ball. The England manager, Roy Hodgson, calls this "front foot defending" and believes that without it, your team will find it very difficult to provide a threat on the counter.

2. **Take Away The Screener** – Most teams today employ a holding midfielder or 'screener' to prevent counter attacks. Once you win the ball, the first player in possession has a decision to make - dribble or pass. They make this decision with the screener in mind. If they can play or dribble the ball beyond the holding midfielder, the defensive ball line will be exposed and they usually retreat, creating more space for your team to penetrate. The majority of defensive midfielders are not blessed with speed so once they are out of the first phase, they usually find it difficult to recover.

3. **Influence The Center Backs** – Once you remove the 'screener', the center backs become the target. They will want to work as a pair, with one dropping and one stepping, but require time to make this decision. Attackers who put them under pressure and drive at them with the ball are usually rewarded. Again, the front three of Barcelona are a great example of this with each fully capable of beating the center back in a 1v1 situation or combining with each other.

4. **Win The Race** – This is where the choice of language can make a real difference in coaching young players. If you ask them to push up and support the attack, they probably will be reluctant to do it because it is an awful lot of work, and you may not be rewarded. However, if you ask them to "Win the race", their competitive juices will flow and it becomes a phase of the game which they can directly influence. Remember, we must 'sell' ideas to our players and how we word our coaching points can make a difference in how they are interpreted.

Exercise One

As we have previously identified, counter attacking works best when you can provide numbers in support and create overloads in the final third. This exercise creates a game-like situation that challenges all players to work at their maximum, both with and without the ball. Physically, if just one player is lagging behind, it will have tactical repercussions as no overload will be created and therefore the chances of scoring will be dramatically decreased. It also works on the trigger to start, which Sir Alex Ferguson believes is the key to fast transitions, "the first pass forward – an accurate pass forward, which allows players to sprint forward in support of the ball – is very important."

The game takes place on a full field and the players are split into three teams of four. Before the game, you can organize them in any kind of system, both in and out of possession. By giving each team tactical instructions, you are holding them accountable for positions they must take up later in the exercise, which will be important when fatigue becomes a factor. In addition, there are two all-time target forwards who stay in each offensive third.

The game starts with one team of four (black and white stripes below) along with a target forward attacking another group of five players (white team) in one of the attacking thirds. The team in possession attack in a 5v4 situation and have ten seconds to score. If they are successful, they get another ball from the halfway line and attack the other goal. If the defensive team (white team) is successful and wins the ball, then the counter attack is triggered. They must work the ball to the target forward on the other side with a direct pass or a series of short passes. The same 5v4 situation then takes place under the same conditions of ten seconds to score. With the time restrictions, the game is a series of transitions that should be played at a high tempo. Play three sets of four minute games and always keep the score.

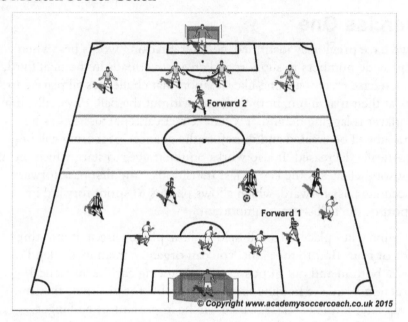

Progressions:

- If the goalkeeper makes a save, they must play short to the defensive team in order to build and play out of the back. This challenges the team in possession to create angles and the team out of possession to press.
- Teams are only allowed three touches in the middle zone. This will make transitions quicker and will not allow players any opportunity to take a break in the counter.
- Encourage players not to support the ball sideways or square, but rather to get ahead of the ball and create depth in the attack.
- You can organize the teams of four differently from one another so the defensive groups are challenged to play against a variety of systems in each attack.
- One of the target forwards can drop into the middle zone to receive the ball. This gets them into the habit of checking towards the ball. It may be a good idea to limit their touches when they do that in order to keep the speed of play as high and realistic as possible.
- Add a time limit for teams to play out of the back. If they are unsuccessful in doing so, possession goes back to the team which was initially attacking.

Exercise Two

When we watch counter attacking at the highest level, we can sometimes be forgiven for focusing on the distances players cover and the speed at which they turn defense into attack. We must remember, however, that the quality of decision making and final product is what defines the counter. This exercise focuses on efficiency and creating the chance on goal in an overload situation. Counter attacking is not just about running forward, as players must be aware of the angles of support and also remain onside. It is a great exercise for attacking players to get practice in penetration towards goal, and also has a transition element... so quick thinking and intelligent movement are rewarded.

Players are organized in a 25x50 yard area and start with two defenders (white shirts) and three attackers (black shirts). The attacking team begins the exercise in a 3v2 situation towards goal. As soon as the black team finishes on goal, the trigger for the transition begins. A player from the white team dribbles onto the pitch, the two white defenders become attackers, and the black team must lose a player in their transition to the defensive side. Play 3x4 minutes and always keep the score.

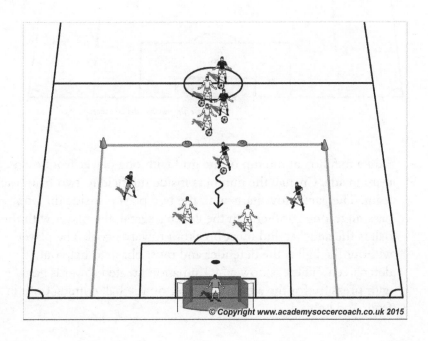

© Copyright www.academysoccercoach.co.uk 2015

Progressions:

- Add a time limit of 7 seconds for the attacking team to create the opportunity on goal.
- Change the starting point for the player who dribbles onto the field. This will change the starting point of the attack and challenge players in their movement and angles of support.
- Add a defensive line at the top (see below) where the defensive team can attempt to dribble through if they win possession. This should lift the competitive nature of the exercise.

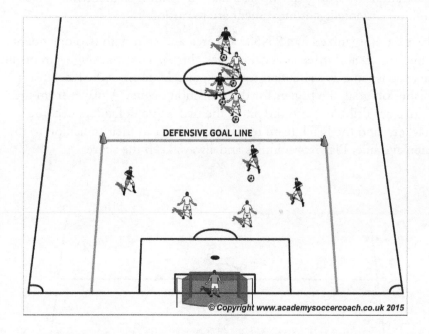

DEFENSIVE GOAL LINE

© Copyright www.academysoccercoach.co.uk 2015

- Add a 5x5 box at the top of the grid with one player from each team inside. Change the numbers inside the field to two from each team. The game now starts with the two players inside the box passing to one another. On the coach's signal, the player with the ball is the attacker and must breakout towards goal. The player without the ball is the defender and must chase to help out defensively. There is now a 3v3 situation created towards goal with pressure for the attacking player on the ball coming both in front and behind.

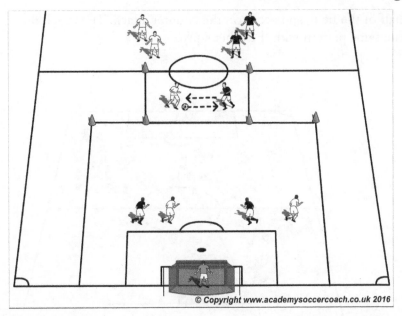

© Copyright www.academysoccercoach.co.uk 2016

Exercise Three

Counter attacking is not simply limited to central areas and many teams have enjoyed success from breaking along the flanks. It used to be the trademark of Manchester United under Sir Alex Ferguson with Giggs and Kanchelskis in the early 1990s, and then Ronaldo and Nani in more recent years. Although wide areas are more difficult to attack through, teams usually find more space and less defensive cover. This exercise targets winning the ball back in one of the flanks, playing off the center forward, and getting supporting midfielders to provide support and take advantage of attacking overloads. You also don't have a holding midfielder to deal with so players can find space more easily. If you watch Atletico Madrid under Diego Simeone, they have been hugely successful in setting defensive traps in wide areas so that they can break and exploit defensive systems which may be out of shape.

The exercise takes place on a full field with 18 players and 2 goalkeepers. There are two 15x15 yard grids located in each half of the field with four players from each team inside both squares. Each team has a center forward and a central defender also located in both halves. The play starts in one square with a 4v4 game. The coach assigns one team to keep possession (white team below). If they keep the ball for 10 consecutive passes, they score a point. As soon as the opposition (black team) wins possession, they are looking to play into their center forward on the other half of the field, and score on the counter attack. The coach then repeats the same pattern with the other square.

© Copyright www.academysoccercoach.co.uk 2015

Progressions:

- Give the attacking team ten seconds to score so they are encouraged to be direct and score quickly.
- Challenge the counter attacking team to only pass the ball forward. This means that supporting runs have to be made ahead of the play, and it becomes physically demanding for the midfielders. The offside rule still applies so timing is important.
- Encourage the midfield players to provide support on both sides of the center forward. The easy option is to run down the line but to really exploit the space on the break, one or more players will need to get on the other side too.
- Limit the center forward to one touch. This challenges the counter attacking team to provide support within seconds. When one player from inside the grid makes the pass into the forward, there should be help on its way instantly.
- Add another center back so they have a covering defender and it becomes more challenging to score.

- Allow the center back to win the ball on the entry pass. This challenges the center forward to look after the ball and will replicate the situation they will find themselves in during a game.
- Defensive team is allowed to have one recovering defender who can come from the 4v4 game.

Exercise Four

How quickly support arrives for the attacking team can make or break counter attacking. If a team fails to provide their forward with help, they become isolated because, in most cases, the defensive team is usually set up with cover to outnumber the attackers. This exercise focuses on turning that initial scenario into an overload in favor of the attacking team and is where the best counter attacking teams thrive. The exercise is also a multi-functional one that challenges attacking players to combine and score in the initial phase, as well as subsequently working at their maximum to provide support and attack in a 4v3 situation towards goal. The exercise is split into two parts, in either half of the field. The defending team works in groups of three (white shirts) and a goalkeeper. The attacking team works in groups of four (see players at cones A, B, C and D).

© Copyright www.academysoccercoach.co.uk 2015

The Modern Soccer Coach

Part one of the exercise involves Players A and B, and a server by the goal with a selection of balls. Player A starts the exercise with a square pass to player B. Player A overlaps Player B, who plays a quick reverse pass and gives Player A the opportunity to have a shot on goal.

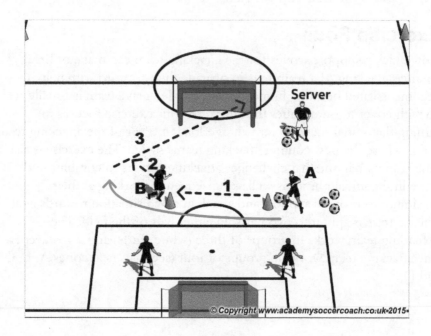

As soon as Player A shoots on goal, Player B receives a pass from Server. Player B must take one touch to open up in possession and then play a long-range pass to Player C or Player D in the other half. This lofted pass has now triggered the beginning of the counter attack. When the ball is on the way to Player C or D, Player A continues the run after their shot on goal and provides support in a central area. There is now a 3v3 situation towards goal. As soon as Player B arrives in the final third, it becomes a 4v3 in favor of the attacking team. There is a 10 second time limit within which the attacking team has to score. This is to make sure they play forward and do not turn the exercise into a possession drill, where it would become unrealistic for a counter attacking session.

© Copyright www.academysoccercoach.co.uk 2015

Progressions:

-   Change the starting point of the three defenders in relation to the goal line. As soon as player B shoots on goal in the first phase of the exercise, the three defenders can then push up and defend.
-   Move the goal used in the first phase back 10 yards, along with the starting points of Player C and D. This gives them more distance to cover and attack towards goal. Encourage players to provide support ahead of the ball in order to challenge them to add depth to the attack.
-   Cut the time on the attack from 10 seconds to 8 seconds. This should increase the intensity levels of the exercise.
-   Give wide attackers a number (one or two). As soon as the server passes the ball to player A, he/she shouts out a number and player A must then set the ball in the direction of that player and then provide a long range pass.
-   Replace Server with a defender who passes the ball to Player A and then immediately applies pressure. Player A can choose to beat the defender in a 1v1 situation, pass quickly to players D or C, or combine with player B. This adds a decision making component to the exercise.

- Change from three defenders to four defenders. The situation then becomes a 4v4 and should provide a huge challenge to the attacking team.
- Add a goalkeeper in the first phase and challenge the attacking team to score a certain number of goals in a set time. You can award one point for a goal in the first phase and two points for a goal in the second phase.

Exercise Five

Creating attacking overloads is the focal point of this exercise. As we have already discussed in this chapter, if the attacking team can provide support quicker than the time the opposition takes to get organized, the chances of creating a goalscoring opportunity are greatly increased. More numbers in the attack puts defenders on the back foot and asks the opposition big questions about their ability to regain shape and get compact. This exercise not only challenges the supporting players to provide help to the target forward as quickly as possible, but also works on the width and depth of the support. Players must have an understanding and appreciation of space and there is no point in creating an attacking overload if all the attacking players do so in a congested area. Here, we are looking to exploit space as much as we are looking to exploit overloads. The possession element to the exercise acts as a quality control mechanism and keeps the standards high in terms of passing.

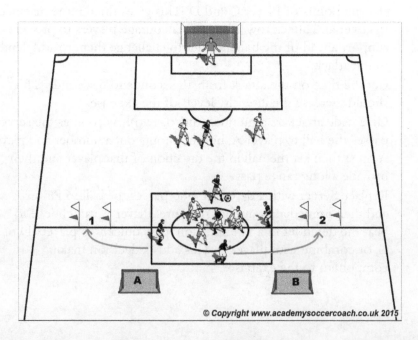

The exercise takes place on a full field with 11 field players and a goalkeeper. The team in black shirts is organized with five midfielders and a target forward, whereas the team in white shirts is set up with three midfielders and two central defenders. The exercise starts with a 5x3 possession game inside a 15x15 yard square. The aim of the team in possession is to complete five successive passes and then play into the center forward. As soon as they pass the ball into the center forward, two midfielders can break from the grid in support, but must do so firstly by running through the flags at 1 and 2. If they do this at maximum speed, they should create a 3v1 situation to goal within seconds. If the defensive team (white) win the ball inside the square, they can score by passing into mini-goals labelled A and B.

Progressions:

- Provide a starting point for the center forward and two defenders that restricts their movement before the ball is played into the forward. The objective here is to prevent the forward from starting close enough to the possession grid where the supporting players are.
- Alter the starting points of the flags at 1 and 2, so the players have to cover more ground before support arrives.
- After 5 seconds, allow one or two players from the black team inside the possession grid to recover and act as defenders.
- After 7 seconds, the entire square can join in the second phase. If the defensive team wins possession, they can still play into goals A and B. This then challenges the attacking team to apply counter pressure once the ball is lost.

Exercise Six

Counter attacking opportunities are multiplied when you are playing against a team who build through the defensive and midfield thirds in possession. A possession-based team will play short passes that will test the speed and quality of pressing, as well as the ability to turn defense into attack. In this 7v7 game, two teams work on alternative styles of play; one builds an attack patiently, while the other seeks to punish and destroy immediately. Players are challenged with their shape and system. The game takes place inside an 80x40 yard area, split into three zones. There are six players on each team, plus a goalkeeper. Both teams set up with four players in the midfield area. The team which starts in possession first (black team below), will have two forwards up against two defenders in the final third. No players, other than the keeper, will occupy the first third. Coach starts the exercise by serving the ball to the goalkeeper of the black team. One defender can drop into the defensive third unopposed, to pick up possession and start the build-up phase. The black team must play through the middle grid before they can enter the final third. Once they enter the attacking third, one white player can join the attack to create a 3v2 towards goal. If the black team wins the ball, they are trying to counter right away.

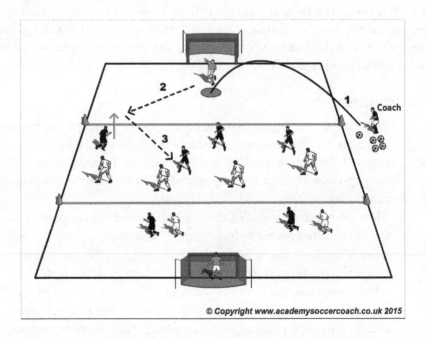

© Copyright www.academysoccercoach.co.uk 2015

Progressions:

- Four players from the counter attacking team must be in the attacking third when they attempt a shot on goal. If they are not, the goal does not count. This adds a sense of urgency to the supporting runs.
- When the black team receives the ball from the goalkeeper, they now have the option of playing through the midfield or directly into the final third.
- The counter attacking team must produce a shot on goal within ten seconds of winning the ball. This will prevent the exercise from becoming a possession game.
- Increase the field size and numbers. This gives both teams more ground to cover and increases physical demands, both defensively and on the counter attack. Below you can see that the full pitch

allows you to set an initial line of pressure where the press is triggered and should allow players to transfer these scenarios to an 11v11 situation.

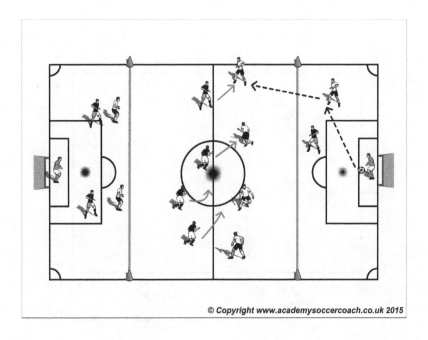

Exercise Seven

The old saying "A team is most vulnerable right after they score" is really put to the test in this exercise. It challenges players' abilities to think quickly, as well as take advantage of time and space. The competitive element of the game also means that recovery runs are fast and players have a limited time to take advantage of overloads towards goal. It is a counter-attacking exercise developed by Alex Schultz, assistant coach at Regis University, and focuses on players going at their maximum, both in and out of possession. The game will be won or lost in the speed of transitions, with high demands on both awareness and speed of decision making.

Players are set up in a 3v3 game on a 20x30 yard pitch with mini-goals. There is a good supply of balls located in each corner of the field. It begins as a basic 3v3 game with no restrictions on the players. Once a goal is scored by either side, the counter attack is triggered. The player who scores the goal must run behind the goal before entering the field again. The team which has just conceded must sprint over to the corner and retrieve one of the balls to create a 3v2 on the counter attack. After three minutes, both teams are replaced by a new 3v3 group and the game continues. Each team plays three sets each and the score keeps going. Competition will drive the intensity of the game even higher.

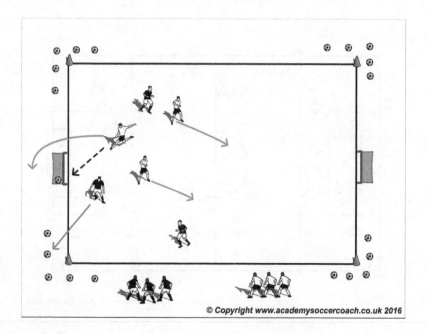

© Copyright www.academysoccercoach.co.uk 2016

Progressions:

- To increase the physical demands on players or give the counter attacking team more time to exploit the numbers advantage, add a cone, pole, or mannequin behind the goal. After scoring, the player now has to run around it, before getting back into the game.
- Add a neutral player who plays with the team in possession. This will create a 4v3 at the start and a 4v2 on the counter attack. The objective of this change is that there should be many more goals scored and therefore more counter attacking opportunities in the 3 minute game.
- Change the dimensions of the pitch to 30x40 yards and replace the mini-goals with full-sized goals, along with a goalkeeper for each team. The game can now either be a 3v3 or 4v4 and defending becomes physically more difficult because of the threat of long distance shots and combination plays.

Exercise Eight

In this exercise, we attempt to change the perception of counter attacking as a negative style of play and move it more towards a different way of pressing. You can see how teams, especially those which do not have elite players, can become somewhat discouraged when they are told about the counter attacking gameplan. It is difficult for teams to create an aggressive mindset if the coach is asking them to drop off and absorb pressure. The reality, however, is that you do not need to counter attack from one penalty box to the other, however spectacular it may look. You can counter higher up the field, and in doing so, raise your chances of scoring as you have less ground to cover and can get help there quicker. This game is designed to show players exactly that difference in counter attacking scenarios and encourage them to take advantage of it. It is a tactical 8v8 game where the focus is on winning the ball, recognizing the cue to counter, and taking advantage of numerical overloads in the attack. The game is conditioned to reward teams winning the ball in higher areas up the field.

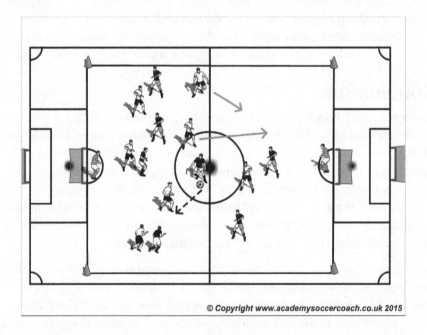

© Copyright www.academysoccercoach.co.uk 2015

The game takes place in an area between both 18-yard boxes. There are eight players on each team, including a goalkeeper. The coach can organize them tactically in any way they choose to do so but may have to manipulate the game slightly if either team chooses to set up with high numbers defensively. One team attacks normally (black shirts) towards the opposition goal. They have no restrictions to their play in possession. The other team (white shirts) looks to counter attack as soon as they win possession and have a time limit of 10 seconds to score.

Here is the key to the session: as soon as the white team wins the ball, the black team can only defend with those players who were behind the ball at that time. This means that defensive players cannot recover and the rewards of winning the ball higher up the field is a lot greater. With this game condition, success for the counter attacking team lies in where they win the ball and how quickly they can get players involved. After 4 minutes, both teams switch roles.

Progressions:

- Increase the size of the field to full field. This creates more ground to cover.
- Decrease the counter-attacking time from 10 seconds to 8 seconds.
- Add a condition to the game where a certain number of counter attacking players must be within a set distance for the goal to count. Again, you want to challenge players to make the runs to get involved rather than sit back and watch the forwards do it.

Conclusion

There are many hurdles to overcome in order to consistently be successful at counter attacking. The defensive structure of some teams is not strong enough, while others struggle with the execution of skills at crucial moments in the final third. The biggest challenge to successfully implement with your team, however, will always be the physical commitment required to win the ball back and then sprint long distances at full speed to support the attack, aware that you may not even touch the ball but instead providing a decoy for another attacker.

How do you get your players to make those lung-busting runs over and over again, without complaint or fatigue? This level of physical output needs to be driven by both your sessions and your culture from day one. When players are fresh and willing to go above and beyond in pre-season, don't waste their energy running around a track or up hills. Instead have them experiencing these scenarios time and time again at full speed. Timing is so important because, early in pre-season, players do not even see this as work. They see competitive, game-like situations that allow them to express themselves and show what they can do. Therefore it is an optimal time for coaches to set the foundation for how they will implement the principles of counter attacking in games and what standard is required of each player. Once players are aware of this, the majority of them will not want to let your team down and that is why the best counter attacking teams become so effective on the break.

4

Pressing

One criticism directed at the modern game is that coaches can be led to believe that there are new concepts emerging that have never before existed. Pressing is one theme that has really come alive in recent years with the success of Barcelona under Pep Guardiola and Borussia Dortmund with Jurgen Klopp.

Of course, experienced coaches and ex-pros scoff at that idea and will happily remind you that pressing has been around for many years. The 'Total Football' philosophy, developed by Rinus Michels and Holland during the 1974 World Cup, reshaped the global view of defending, as well as possession. We learned that it was not simply about stopping players through physical force, but that teams could *work together* to become highly effective.

Over ten years later, Arrigo Sacchi evolved this model further during his work with Italy and AC Milan and produced a style of soccer that almost defined an era. His meticulous preparation, combined with the Italian love of defending, meant that players moved in relation to the ball, the entire team would step and drop together, and distances between lines of confrontation and defense were both compact and set in stone. As coaches from around the world watched with admiration, a new defensive foundation was set and the game would never be the same. Fast forward twenty years, add new laws that allow attacking players to flourish more, as well as a brand of athlete that can cover distance quickly, and you now have a new and improved version of defending for teams to both learn and master.

So have modern coaches like Klopp, Simeone, Sampaoli, and Pochettino invented pressing? Absolutely not. However, I believe that they have found a way to do it efficiently and effectively in a game that is significantly different to any previous generation, and therefore deserve all the credit that comes their way because of it. Former Newcastle United coach, John Carver, claimed recently that pressing was the "easiest thing to coach in football." I would argue that it's actually the toughest because of the complex variables associated with it.

Firstly, the technical ability of defenders today is higher than ever before. Good defenders have the ability to break pressure with a pass; great defenders have the ability to break pressure by 'stepping out' and beating an opponent. Secondly, and possibly most importantly, pressing needs to be almost perfect to work. One mistake and the whole defensive system can be exposed.

Barcelona coach, Luis Enrique, echoes the belief that there is no such thing as half measures with this style of play. "It has to be done by all 11 players, otherwise it doesn't work. The players must move in formation together. A great coach must convince their players to believe in this vision and make sure they do. If a player only does it because the trainer says so, that's not good enough! The players must believe."

Before deciding to adopt a system that involves high pressing, a coach must be aware of why they are trying to pressure the ball, and not simply choosing the pressing style because it's in vogue. Some of the major advantages of effective pressing are that it:

- Controls the tempo of the game.
- Breaks attacking patterns of the opposition.
- Speeds the opposition up, and forces them to play at a tempo which they are not comfortable with.
- Can change the focus of your opponent so they are more concerned about keeping possession than they are about starting an attack.
- Huge rewards! Winning the ball higher up the field allows you to be closer to the opponent's goal with their defensive unit disorganized.

Coaching the Press

As Luis Enrique said, once you decide to implement pressing to your playing system, you have to get it right. Before you even start, however, you must be aware that not every player will necessarily want to do it. It may be an exciting style to watch but there is a reason why Southampton players joked that they required "two hearts and three lungs" when they played for Mauricio Pochettino. It takes phenomenal commitment and pushes players to the very edge, both physically and mentally. Every player, therefore, must have the required appetite for hard work, possess the capabilities to both understand and apply it, and then have the ability to execute it. Yes, it does take ability too! This is about much more than physical work.

Pressing as an Individual

Without the ability to make the correct decisions, a player who presses relies solely on speed and aggression, which alone does not guarantee success. The higher the level, the more intelligence is required from the pressing team and the greater the consequences if they get it wrong. I believe that this aspect of pressing is overlooked by a lot of coaches and we tend to generalize our players as having great 'game intelligence' or lacking it. Instead it is about awareness, focus, and identifying triggers – all of which can be coached. Before deciding to press, each player must make the following decisions:

1.   Which player do I leave in order to go and press?
2.   What angle do I approach from?
3.   What is the risk-reward of going to press?
4.   Where do I recover to after pressing?

Pressing as a Team

No team in the world can press continuously, at a high level, for 90 minutes. It is just not physically possible and players will always need time to recover. Even Barcelona requires a 'breather' every now and again, although it's usually when they are in possession of the ball. For teams who do not have the luxury of using possession as a method of recovery, they need to pick and choose their moments of when to press and when not to. If some players press and others do not, gaps open and the shape of the team will get ripped apart. This is where the use of 'triggers' comes in.

Triggers are important because they allow players to identify moments in the game when they can press as a team. It keeps everyone on the same page and develops an understanding of the defensive system. Jed Davies, author of 'Coaching The Tika-Taka Style of Play' and 'The Philosophy of Football: In Marcelo Bielsa's Shadows', has studied pressing in the modern game for a number of years. His research has found that, at Southampton, Mauricio Pochettino had fifteen pressing triggers for his players. Now that is a complex system! With the understanding that not all coaches are working with Premier League caliber professionals, Davies looked to simplify this and broke pressing triggers down to four main categories.

1. The attacking team is not yet organized/ yet to transition into a shape that supports ball retention. This is a really aggressive reaction to losing possession and there are a variety of ways to do it. Barcelona caused havoc with their '6 Second Rule' (try and regain the ball in six seconds or less) on the rare occasions that possession was given away. Another trigger to press aggressively is if defenders outnumber attackers in the area that the ball has been lost, or if it is a 1v1 situation. Both situations mean that the team in possession does not have a lot of options so are more vulnerable to conceding possession at that time.

2. The opposition's conditions for control are not present or are yet to be created. This is an opportunity to press that is caused by favorable circumstances for the defensive team, such as a bad pitch, a bouncing ball, a slow pass, a backwards pass, or when an opponent receives the ball under uncomfortable conditions (e.g. on their weaker foot or with a square body shape).

3. Patterned traps. A number of top teams force the ball wide and then set about pressing aggressively. This is because space is at a premium and teams in possession only have one direction in which to play out. Pep Guardiola once famously stated "The touchline is the best defender in the world." His Barcelona and Bayern Munich teams have excelled in showing teams into wide areas and pouncing on them.

4. Pressure in relation to risk. Jed Davies believes that teams who press high up the pitch have three different approaches, depending on where the action is taking place. These are man-to-man pressing, zonal pressing, and option-based pressing. Man-to-man typically follows the rule of the 'nearest man' closing the opponent down and forcing them to play a long ball out of pressure. Zonal pressing is when the pressing team forces play into a defensively overloaded area and usually takes place around the midfield area. Option-based pressing forces play into a predictable area, where the defending team invite the pass into the only option left open. It is often the basis for setting traps in different areas of the field.

Exercise One

An aggressive mentality is so important to pressing, but even more important is how you attempt to achieve it. The coach definitely plays a part here and it is no coincidence that most pressing teams play under coaches who are highly animated on the touchline. The training environment also plays a key role in communicating this intensity and urgency towards the players. In fact, I believe there is a strong correlation between the two. Any time I have visited clubs and observed training, I am always keen to see how the first ten minutes of the session develops and then I question whether there is a link to their style of play. Nine

The Modern Soccer Coach

times out of ten they are a mirror image of each other. Everything from the warm-up onwards plays a role. The slow starters in training typically have the tempo of the game dictated to them by the opposition and vice versa. This was a theme we focused on in 'The Modern Soccer Coach 2014' and certainly applies to pressing and building a team who can play on the front foot every game. This exercise is perfect to start a session during the preseason program because the nature of it will naturally switch players to 'game mode' almost immediately.

The exercise takes place inside a 15x15 yard area with 12 players divided into three teams of four. One team starts as the possession team (black), another as the pressing team (white), and the third team recovers. Once the coach signals, the possession team starts passing a ball inside the area. The first player on the pressing team must do some short, explosive footwork at the cones and then sprint through the gate and attempt to win the ball back in a 4v1 situation. As soon as he/she enters the area, the next player from the pressing team goes, and so on. So, inside the square, you can eventually progress to a 4v4.

The scoring system works by giving the possession team 30 seconds to keep the ball, regardless of the numbers. This should give all four pressing players an opportunity to get in and try to win the ball back as quickly as possible. If the possession team is successful at keeping the ball for 30 seconds, the pressing team switches with the recovery team and the possession team stays. However, if the pressing team is successful and wins the ball back before 30 seconds, the teams rotate.

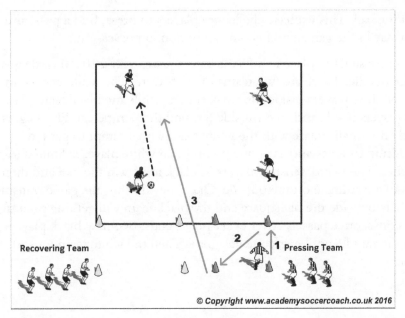

© Copyright www.academysoccercoach.co.uk 2016

Progressions:

- Add a technical station for the recovery team so they keep working at a low intensity.
- Manipulate the speed work with the pressing team by increasing distances or adding poles.
- Increase the time to 1 minute but increase the playing area too. This will put more emphasis on pressing as a four and hunting in packs.

Exercise Two

So many players get frustrated when they are instructed to press, not because they cannot win the ball, but because they do not know what to do with it, or have few options, once they win it. Hence, they give it right back and have to start again. This exercise teaches players to understand the difference between closing down and pressing. Closing down is when you apply pressure in order to stop your opponents from easily building an attack. We've all seen the center forward who wastes energy chasing the back pass to the goalkeeper, knowing they will never get there, while their nearest teammate is over 50 yards away. Pressing is rather different. Teams who press do so because it creates an opportunity which they can exploit in a dangerous area of the field. You cannot press effectively without having an attacking mentality and an idea of what you want to do with the ball. This exercise challenges players to press, find a pass, and then stay in the game and become an option in possession.

The exercise takes place in a 25x25 yard square, with a 10x10 yard square in the middle. There are two teams of six players. The white team start with all their players inside the small square, while the black team place two players inside and four outside (around the perimeter). Play begins inside the small square with the white team who attempt to get ten consecutive passes and earn one point. Each white player is limited to two touches. The two defensive players in black must win the ball and then pass to a teammate on the outside. Once they do this, the game transitions into a 6v6 inside the big square and the black team will get one point for five consecutive passes. After every phase ends, two new black players go into the middle until everyone has gone. Then the white team must do the same.

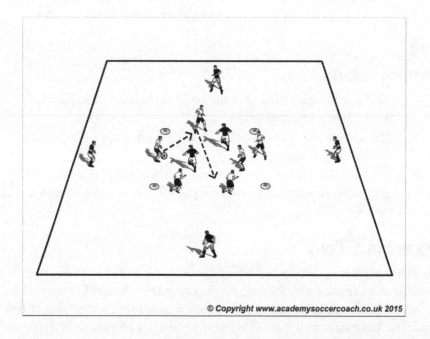

Progressions:

- The two defensive players in the middle must work together. They should attempt to 'show' the player in possession back to where they came from and don't allow one pass to split them (see above). Award the team in possession an automatic goal for one split and see if you can incentivize the defensive players to work as a unit.

- Manipulate the pass totals by increasing or decreasing the totals needed for points. This can add an intensity to the game and the more competitive it is, the higher the tempo that will be created.

- Only allow four defensive white players to leave the small square once they lose positon and the game transitions the other way. By lowering the numbers, you increase the physical demands and add a counter pressing element to the game.

- A tactical progression of this exercise has been developed by Neil Adair. The exercise now takes place on a half-field with the outside players located in the corners. The same principles apply in the middle, but when a defender presses, wins the ball, and plays to the outside (below), the exercise then transitions into a 6v6 towards goal.

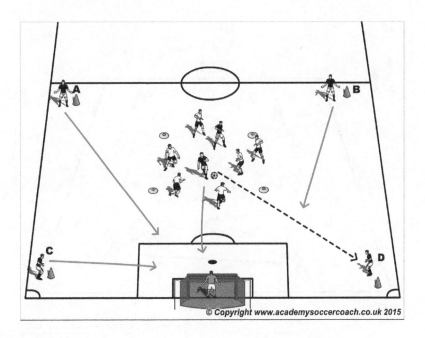

Exercise Three

During the preseason period, you need to build up the fitness levels of players who are going to adopt the pressing style during the game. You cannot expect them to walk on the field and perfect it right away. This exercise allows the defensive team to recover for short periods of time, so that the intensity of defensive work can almost always be kept at a high level. It also rewards a pressing team for their ability to play after they win the ball, rather than simply stopping the team in possession. In addition, there are both transitional and competitive elements which also keep the tempo high throughout.

The exercise takes place inside a 20x20 area, with four goals on the outside. There are twelve players involved, with two teams of six players. The white shirts begin in possession with all six players, while the black shirts start with three players working defensively and three players recovering. The rules are straightforward. The white team is looking to make 10 consecutive passes to score a point and the black team is aiming to win possession and score in any of the four goals, which is worth two points. The game lasts for three minutes and then the defensive team rotates immediately. After both defensive units work, teams switch roles and the white teams goes on defense. Play four sets and always keep the score.

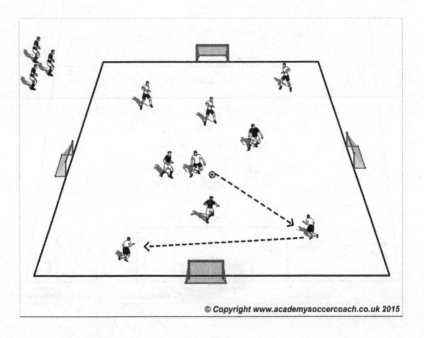

Progressions:

- The size of the playing area can be manipulated to increase or decrease physical demands for the defenders.

- Imposing a one or two touch restriction will allow the defensive team to become more aggressive with their pressing because there is no way to be beaten on the dribble.
- Add a technical station as part of the recovery where players now have to work on basic technique as they are tired. This will keep them engaged and also increases the difficulty level of the exercise.
- Change the set-up to three teams of four players each (see below). One team (stripes) presses all the time and they must play against both the black and white shirts combined in an 8v4 situation. Teams are tested on their ability to press – if they win the ball they get a point for scoring in one of the goals and if the other teams combine for ten consecutive passes, the pressing team loses a point. Play lasts for four minutes and then another team must take the place of the pressers. The ball always starts from the outside and gives the pressing team a different starting point that they must adjust to at every restart.

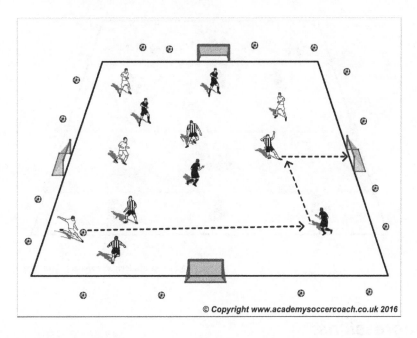

© Copyright www.academysoccercoach.co.uk 2016

Exercise Four

We have already identified that effective pressing takes discipline and the ability to make quick defensive decisions, not just running and closing down. If an unorganized team decides to press, they usually get taken apart quite easily. This exercise focuses on zones and challenges players to move intelligently instead of just aggressively, and make smart decisions rather than just chase the ball. The players are organized into two teams of six, with three players of each team in every alternate zone. There is one neutral player (in stripes) who plays for whatever team has possession of the ball. All players must stay in their designated area, except the neutral player, who is free to go into any zone with possession of the ball. Teams score a point by transferring the ball from one zone to another. The ball must remain below knee-height so no lofted passes over defenders. The neutral player can be used to help score a point and creates a challenge for the defensive team, as you can see in the diagram below, because he/she can play beneath the pressing line and receive the ball to score a point. Therefore, teams must not only be compact but must also prevent the neutral player from receiving the ball in dangerous positions. This takes work, communication, and focus – all requirements of effective pressing.

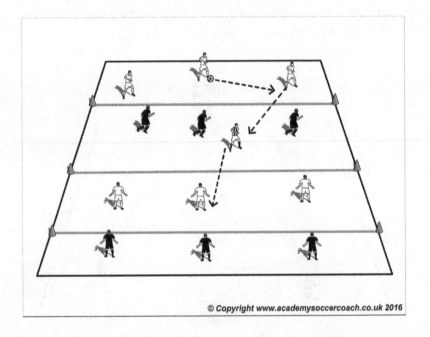

© Copyright www.academysoccercoach.co.uk 2016

Progressions:

- Create a touch limit so the ball moves faster and players must make quicker decisions both in and out of possession.
- Introduce a maximum pass limit of four in each zone so that teams will try to play forward more and allow pressing to be more aggressive.
- Change from four zones to three and create three teams of four players (see below). Now two players on the defensive team

(stripes) are allowed out of their zone to press the ball. The two remaining players must shift and try to intercept the penetrating pass for a point. In this game, the team in possession must have a minimum of five consecutive passes before they can transfer the ball and score a point. There is a transition element to the game so the team who can adjust after a point is scored or possession is lost, will be successful.

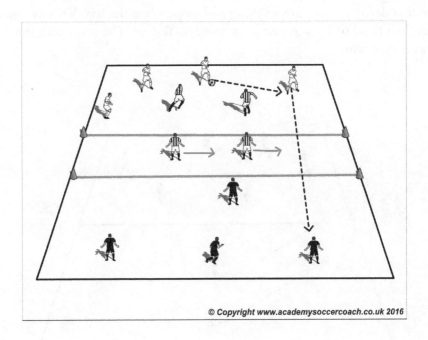

Exercise Five

There is no doubt that pressing works best in tight areas. Defensively, it accommodates intensity and maximum effort. However, nothing kills it more than the switch. You can almost see the energy drain from teams when they go hunting in packs, looking to trap a team in an area, only for the opposition to open up the entire pitch, escape, and attack with a defense that is out of balance. This exercise works on pressing to prevent the switch and either teaches, or reminds players, how devastating it can be tactically and physically if you let the opposition open up the field. This is where small defensive margins can become huge ones. By not putting in sufficient intensity when pressing early, defensive players can multiply their own workloads later and it can have a dramatic snowball effect.

In this exercise, eighteen players are organized into three teams. Two teams occupy two 15x15 yard square areas. The third team is organized into pairs. Play starts from a coach who passes the ball into one of the squares. The team in possession is aiming to get ten consecutive passes inside their area, and then transfer the ball to the other square. Defenders work in pairs and, if they win the ball, the coach serves a new one to the other side. Each defending pair must win three balls back before the next pair can go. The scoring works on a time system. The clock starts when the first defensive pair are working and stops when the last defensive pair win their third ball. Each pair goes twice on the set. The team with the lowest time wins.

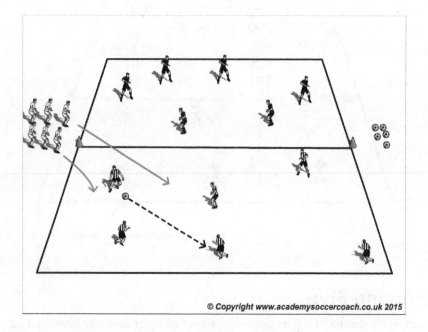

© Copyright www.academysoccercoach.co.uk 2015

Progressions:

- If the team in possession switches the play after ten consecutive passes, coach adds another ball to the defensive pair's workload. Therefore, stopping the switch must be a priority for the defenders.
- If the defensive pair gets split, the coach adds another ball to the defensive pair's workload. This challenges them to stay organized and communicate when they are fatigued.

- Change the pass limits to six or eight before the switch and see if you can increase the urgency of the exercise as players begin to tire.

Exercise Six

If you want to press aggressively with your team, you must develop the mind-set that every player must work at their maximum. They cannot simply rely on their teammates, or try to take some time off. This exercise challenges players to keep their defensive standards high and exposes those who do not. It is a fantastic way to create situations in preseason where players must take responsibility and hold each other accountable in order for the team to be successful. I first saw this exercise from Nate Lie when I was at University of Cincinnati. Because of the competitive setup, within minutes the intensity of the session had reached new levels. Players were redefining what pressing actually was and the communication levels had increased significantly.

The exercise takes place in a 30x15 yard area with two teams. Players on each team have three starting points and the game is a 3v3 with a twist – there are no goalkeepers. When the coach serves the ball to any player and starts the exercise, the pressing should already have started. The players must close down their opponent as soon as possible and not give them room to shoot. There is one restriction – the first player in possession cannot shoot immediately, otherwise it would turn into a one-touch shooting exercise. Instead, after the first player passes to a teammate it is a high intensity 3v3 game with no keepers. Play three sets of 5 minute games and, after each set, allow the players to have one minute where they can reorganize and talk about how they need to press more effectively.

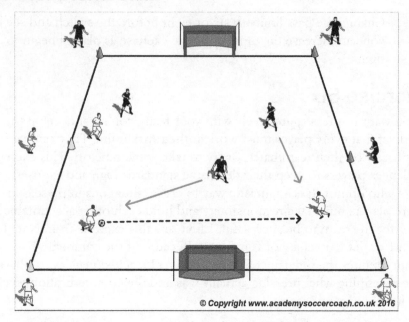

© Copyright www.academysoccercoach.co.uk 2016

Progressions:

- Remove the initial pass rule so that the first player can now shoot once they receive the ball. However, serve everything in the air and allow the defensive players enough time to get there and influence the play if they do so at their maximum speed.
- Keep the same 3v3 group on the pitch for two sets in a row. As soon as the first ball goes out, the coach can serve the second ball to anyone on the pitch. This will challenge players to transition and not simply press the first ball and then stop.
- Create a new scoring system where two points are awarded for a team who can press, win possession, and then score. This will incentivize an even more aggressive style of pressing.

Exercise Seven

It is important that tactical pressing sessions are also part of the pre-season program. Players need to be able to associate the triggers that will arise in a game and how their position changes in relation to the ball. This is an exercise which Pep Guardiola used with his Bayern Munich squad to work on pressing the opposition fullback in possession, high up the field.

The set-up is simple and features an 8v8 game, played from 18 yard box to 18 yard box, with two 'floating players' who play with the team in possession. Teams can score in three goals – the white team scores in goals 1, 2, 3 and the black team scores in goals 4, 5, 6. The tactical element of the game is centered around the location of the outside goals. The position of the goals creates an incentive for teams to press high and in wide areas. If the team is organized in a 3-2-3, the outside forwards can press aggressively high up the field. The role of the two floating players creates an overload for the attacking team so the defenders cannot simply play man-to-man and instead have problems to solve. This, along with the size of the field, means that decisions have to be made quickly and effectively. In an exercise like this, ineffective pressure will result in the attacking team using their numerical advantage and exposing another area of the field – just like a real game.

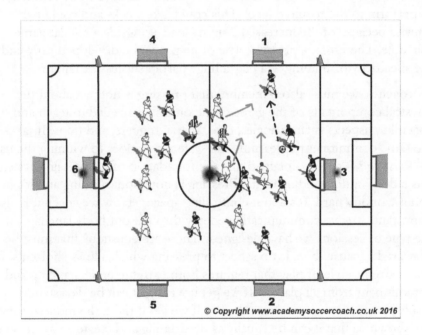

© Copyright www.academysoccercoach.co.uk 2016

Progressions:

- Give the two floating players specific roles to play on either team and then challenge teams to solve problems when they are out of possession. For example, if there are two attacking midfielders, you will have an overload in the middle and will have to defend a lot more compactly or drop numbers in to deal with it.
- Remove the two floating players and play without them. This means teams can be a lot more aggressive and take risks with their pressing.

- Eventually progress to 11v11 and coach within the game. Teams must identify triggers as to when they go and press, and you will see how much information players can take onto a full game.

Conclusion

A team cannot choose to adopt a pressing style and expect to be successful without taking full advantage of the preseason period. The physical demands are so high and complex that players are not naturally conditioned to sustain an effective pressing style for 90 minutes when they enter preseason. Likewise, if a coach decides to implement a pressing system midway through the season, the players have been conditioned to work with entirely different intensity levels and will have to be re-trained to perform to the required level. This could take weeks and could risk injuries because of the increased training load alongside a regular game schedule. Therefore, a pressing style of play must be developed early and the specificity of training will play a huge part in success or failure.

As coaches, we must also remember that pressing is not just about the physical components of the game. Time on task is needed to teach and coach key aspects such as angles, cues, shape, triggers, and traps. It takes the same commitment to learning the system as it does to winning the ball back. Arrigo Sacchi maintained that the foundation of his pressing system was a deep understanding of it. "Pressing is not about running and it's not about working hard. It's about controlling space." How we coach it is also important. Are we communicating energy through our body language or the type of sessions we have designed? These are questions that must be answered because there is no aspect to pressing which allows shortcuts. It is an extreme style of play that requires both extreme understanding and commitment from all players. If we get it wrong, it can be devastating to results, performances, and morale. But if we get it right, the modern game has shown us that it can be equally as devastating and create an aggressive, winning mentality that can set our teams apart both on and off the field.

5

Games-Based Training

Remember in Chapter One when we visited two teams where the difference in their culture and subsequent attitude to preseason training led them down two completely different paths? Even before they started, you could tell which team was going to have a great training session and which one was going to struggle.

Although almost every coach appreciates the value of a highly motivated set of players, an important step in the process of culture creation during preseason is to understand exactly how it can be created. Traditionally, the onus was on the players to set the culture. They were expected to show up with the correct attitude and be prepared to work at their maximum at all times. If they failed to "bring it", the threat of extra work or punishing runs typically brought it out eventually. However, as the game (and society) has changed over the past ten years, we have seen a shift in the spectrum towards the coach setting the tone through enthusiasm and the quality of his/her communication.

The best coaches in the modern game do not create the culture for their players, they work alongside them to co-create a model that will sustain high levels of work from the first day of preseason to the last game of the season.

Culture has nothing to do with luck or the luxury of working with the best players. High energy teams possess incredible levels of enthusiasm and drive largely because they have a strong sense of purpose about their training. They are aware of what is required to operate at a successful level and are not afraid to embrace it and push themselves to new limits. They also realize that they must go above and beyond when 'off the field' too, both in terms of preparation and recovery. The role of the coach therefore is twofold: firstly, they must communicate clearly to their players exactly where the team is going, how they will get there, and what is required. Once the "where, what, and how" are clearly established, players can identify their "why" together, which is typically found to be the fuel that drives successful teams. An incredibly strong sense of purpose and direction can take teams beyond the ordinary and taps into hidden reserves of determination and passion. That is why Atletico Madrid has outperformed neighbors Real Madrid in recent years. Their "why" is stronger than money and high profile players.

The second important role that the coach must play is to facilitate this hunger and drive by creating the best environment possible for the team to work in every day. This includes training that can be easily associated with the game itself.

In this chapter, we will look at games-based training, where possibly the strongest relationship between the game and training is developed.

Preseason benefits

It is not easy for a coach to add games-based training to their preseason program. We are usually armed with a mountain of tactical information that we want the players to absorb and process. In addition, players are never at their best either technically or physically so if either cause the session to break down, coaches have the urge to step in and fix it with structured and repetitive work.

That is what we are taught to do on coaching courses, but it may actually be detrimental during the preseason period. What is good for players technically is sometimes not good for them physically or mentally. A session that is heavy on coaching points tends to move quite slowly and will not prepare players for the type of game that they will face when the season does begin. Here are some of the benefits of implementing games-based training to the preseason program.

Players want to do it – Training that is designed specifically around a game context is every player's dream. They do not feel limited or constricted by 'drills' and feel that they can express themselves in a way they are most comfortable doing. This is exactly what the players want to do when you introduce training; you will always be met with high enthusiasm levels.

Starts a session the right way – As coaches, if we have to go in search of intensity and tempo midway through a session, we will most likely never find it. The sooner the session is sparked into life with the right type of energy – driven from the players – the greater the chance of success. Your challenge for the team and staff is to find ways to sustain energy levels, which is an entirely different game to requesting it.

Easy to complement theme of session – Every session plan should be built around some facet of the playing model. If it cannot be, then it is probably irrelevant. Games-based training should allow players to connect the dots between the playing model and training exercises. This will improve understanding and consistency of the tactical instructions that players will hear on a game day.

Builds competitiveness – There is no greater time for a coach to feed the competitive urge to their team than during preseason. Starting places are up for grabs, new players want to make an impact, and returning players are keen to prove a point. If the competitive levels are high, so too will be tempo and intensity, which in turn will drive technical and physical demands.

Enhances communication – Although many coaches look for team building activities during preseason, best practice may actually be closer to the training pitch than on a ropes course. In my experience, the best way for a team to grow together is by developing a strong, collective work rate on the training pitch. Games based exercises can be conditioned to solve problems, help players work together, and practice winning behaviors – all key components of a successful team.

Creates base for discussions – Communication with the coaching staff is just as important as it is with the players themselves. Coaches can create scenarios in small sided games that allow players to manage the game and see the potential situations that will arise during the real thing. More conversations amongst staff and coaches will strengthen the bond needed to work together during the season.

Practice Design

Of course, it's not just as easy as throwing a ball out and letting the players organize a game amongst themselves. Games-based training should involve the same meticulous levels of planning and preparation that all sessions require.

But, what are the differences between games-based training and just letting players play a match? Quite a few, namely… intensity, focus, challenges directly related to the game model, feedback, and a willingness by the players to act on what they have learned. The last thing you want to do in preseason is waste any time, so the onus is on the coach to make sure that the organization provides their team with the best opportunity to make the most out of the session. In 'The Boot Room' magazine, FA Youth Coach Educator, Ben Barlett, identified four guiding principles when structuring his practices:

Direction – A 'goal' that a team or player attacks. The 'goal' can range from a traditional goal, end zone, or a target player in a target area. It does not have to be opposed. "Every practice should have an element of direction ensuring the principles of attack and defense are fundamental to the practice."

Definition – Ben Barlett believes that the practice "should be constructed within the area of the pitch that it occurs on match day." That way, the exercise will have a "visible definition" to the game. For example, if you are crossing and finishing, the coach should use the full width of the field.

Decisions – Players should have cognitive challenges that ensure the execution of technique is coupled with some kind of visual trigger. The challenges can include decisions to make, problems to solve, or situations to read. The visual triggers can be whether to stay on the ball or release it, showing inside or outside, etc.

Difference – The actions or decisions in the practice present themselves in a distinct way. For example, if the theme of the session is running with the ball, the games can challenge the player in a range of different circumstances, such as dribbling under short and long distances. You can also have different themes for different players in the same session. An example would be one player practicing marking and intercepting, while another practices playing forward.

The design of the pitch also plays an important role for Barlett in the organization of his sessions. In order to save time offering explanations, and players having to learn certain conditions, he always works from four different types of pitch. Taking the pitch size into consideration, alongside session planning, helps complement the theme of the session and can challenge players in a number of different ways. Below are the different types of pitch and the advantages that they serve alongside coaching topics.

1. **Big pitch** – Useful when working on defending, or creating space between units, to play in between or behind. They can also create full game pictures for players with realistic distances that they will encounter in full sized games.

2. **Small pitch** – Excellent way to focus on technical aspects such as first touch and quick interplay, as well as speed of play and thought.

3. **Narrow pitch** – Puts an emphasis to play forward because there is limited space to play around the opposition. Great practice for breaking down a compact defensive block.

4. **Wide pitch** – A pitch that is typically wider than it is long can allow players to focus on switching the play, and both defend and attack in wide areas.

Exercise One

Organization sometimes becomes the biggest challenge for coaches during preseason training. Numbers at practice are usually at their highest and the last thing you want during training is for players to stand around watching and not moving. Also, if you have more than one goalkeeper in the squad, it can be difficult to find ways to get everyone involved and challenged in game-specific ways.

Some coaches send the players who are not involved for a few laps around the field, but this can result in a player's focus dropping, and detract from the intensity of the session. There are ways, however, to solve these problems and manage the workload of all players who attend the session. That is the goal of this exercise.

For the set-up, you have three teams of six players, along with four goalkeepers. Two teams (back and white shirts below) play a 7v7 game on a field from one 18-yard box to the other. The coach can add any conditions on the game. The emphasis may be on pressing, playing out from the back, zones where players are encouraged to create overloads, or even free play.

The team which is not involved (striped shirts) work continuously on a shooting circuit. Players dribble through the cones, shoot on goal, and then get their ball and dribble towards the starting point on the other side. It's important that the players working on the shooting circuit are working at two speeds – recovery and full intensity. When they reach the cones, each player should be working at their maximum and when they are dribbling the ball over to the next station, they should be moving slower and recovering. Two speeds are important because you are physically training them to work on short, dynamic bursts of speed to mirror game demands, rather than continuous slow-steady type running. After four minutes, rotate teams but keep the scores rolling so that competitiveness can help with the tempo of the game.

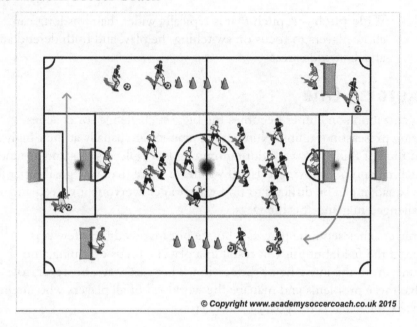

Progressions:

- Coaches can change the conditions of the game or adjust the technical or physical demands of the players on the outside circuit.

- Below is a similar exercise that Jose Mourinho did during a preseason camp with Real Madrid. Mourinho had a lot of staff to help out, so this was how he made use of them with four acting as servers/rebounders, while he coached the game in the middle. There were twenty players split into four teams of five players each. Again, two teams in the middle (black and white shirts) played a possession game with 6 goals. The teams on the outside (A and B) did speed and agility work, combined with combination play and shooting. The first player played a wall pass with a coach, went through the speed ladder, played another wall pass with another coach, accelerated through the mannequins, and then shot on goal. Groups A and B rotated positions.

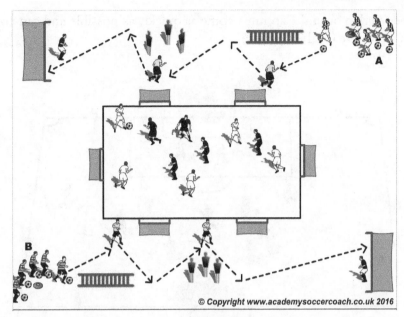

© Copyright www.academysoccercoach.co.uk 2016

Exercise Two

Without a doubt, movement is one of the most important – but under-taught – skills of the game. Coaches scream for it on the sidelines but players (even players at senior level) do not seem to fully understand it. Does it mean move towards the ball, move towards space, or just move anywhere? Of course, the answer can change with every system and every coach. However, with compact defensive units becoming a trademark of the modern game, moving with intent is now becoming a prerequisite for teams and players at the next level.

This game works on the movement of players in wide areas by overlapping and underlapping the player in possession. With more fullbacks today getting forward in the attack, it is a great exercise to build attacking play from wide areas with overloads and speed.

Players are organized into two teams of seven on a 70x50 yard pitch. There are two wide zones on each side, five yards in from the sidelines. Once a team is in possession of the ball, a player can arrive into the wide area. However, the defending team is not allowed in the same channels. Once the ball is passed to a player in a wide channel, they must be overlapped or underlapped by one of their teammates. In order to score, a team must have a cross or combination play from one of the wide channels. The ball is only allowed inside the wide channel for 6 seconds so the overlap or underlap must come as quickly as possible and can come from anywhere on the field.

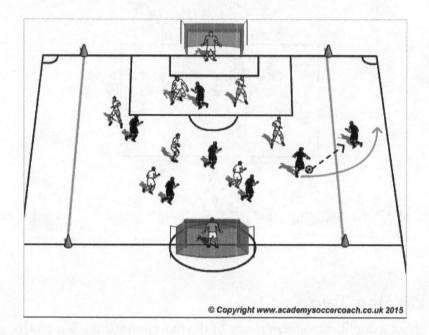

Progressions:

- Allow players to score from free play but create a new points system where teams score one point for an overlap or underlap, two points for a goal, and three points for a combination of both.
- Decrease the time limit needed for the overlap so the focus is on where support comes from. If a forward drifts out to join in the play, another player must take his/her place up front. The movement patterns then progress.
- One defensive player is allowed to come out and defend in a 2v1 situation. Now the execution of the overlap/underlap is challenged and timing becomes a key issue for the pass.

Exercise Three

In March 2016, right before Manchester United played Liverpool in the Europa League, United defender Chris Smalling targeted individual battles as the key to success for his team. "You want to get the upper hand on your opponent, whoever you're playing against. For me, for example, it's the striker. Very early on, you want to get an early challenge in and make sure you dominate."

That type of attitude has played an important part in how a lot of players in the UK have developed and learned the game. You are taught from an early age that you have to "earn the right to play" and that if seven or more players on your team win their individual battles, you are guaranteed to win the game. I heard it a lot growing up and it was a big motivator for me when I played the game because it was simple and easily applicable to my position in central midfield: win the battle here and we should win the game.

Sounds easy.

Of course, if there's one thing the modern game has taught us, it is that physical force alone is not required to win games. The game has developed to a stage where it has become a lot more than a 'battle'. Technical ability and making quick decisions under pressure have moved up the priority list, but players still have to compete and find a way to come out on top.

This game challenges players not just in a physical sense (which is great for preseason) but also in a way where they have to solve problems on both sides of the ball, and take advantage of space with the help of their technical ability.

Fourteen players are divided into two teams of seven, including a goalkeeper on each team. When the teams are made, players must pair up with a player on the opposition who has the same physical qualities as them. The coach may be needed here to mediate and help out. Once the players on each team are paired up, the game can be played. The rules are simple: you can only tackle the player on the other team who you are paired up with – no one else. Players can intercept passes but the essence of the game is you versus your direct opponent. Most players view this in a defensive way, where they do not want to concede, but coaches can turn this game into a fast, attack minded game, where players test the commitment levels of their opponent to track runs and stay tight. Once a player makes a pass, they should be instructed to take a new position ahead of the ball. It can be a phenomenal challenge for players and will reveal a lot about their individual characteristics. Some players will excel, some will not. Play for 3x8 minutes and have a two minute recovery where players can discuss events amongst their team.

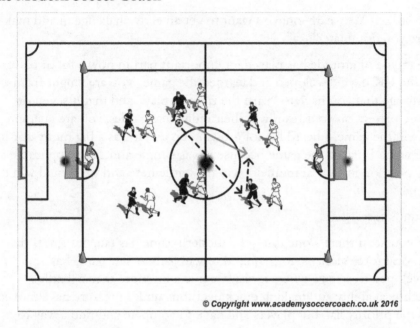

Progressions:

- Have a consequence for the defensive player whose direct opponent scores. It can be pushups or something that they can do quickly to get back into the game. This is designed to increase the competitiveness of the exercise.
- Change the partners after every game. You could even change teams and place your two best competitors against each other.
- Introduce a pass limit before the goal so that the players still understand that it is a team game and are aware of the principles when they are in possession of the ball.

Exercise Four

Sometimes, in a small-sided game, it can be difficult to provide the specific physical demands that the player will see in the game itself. Too often, 6v6 games do not challenge the players to make the same continuous high intensity sprints that they will need to do in a real game. Players have a tendency to get organized and take up familiar positions which lead to the same movements and skills being executed over and over again. The disadvantage here is that if training is always the same, it becomes easier and players get less benefit. Instead, physical and technical improvements require unusual stress through frequent change. Our goal is to break traditional comfort zones and propel players to new levels of physical and technical demands.

The idea for this game came from Neil Adair and is designed to challenge players to transition quickly, recover and press at full intensity, and then play when fatigued.

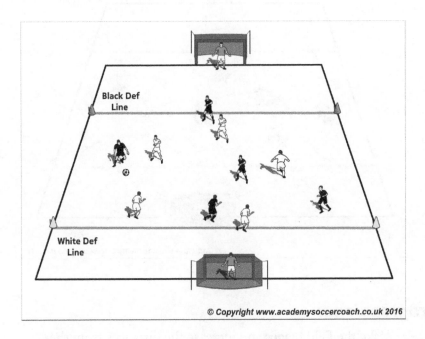

© Copyright www.academysoccercoach.co.uk 2016

Twelve players are split into two teams of five with a goalkeeper on each team. Play takes place in a 20x40 yard area with a defensive line for each team that is located 10 yards from the goal line. There are no restrictions on when the game starts and players can go anywhere on the field.

The only tactical message from the coach before the game starts is that it must be a high pressing encounter. The challenge arrives when a goal is scored. Every player on the team that just scored (black team below) must sprint back to their defensive line and touch it before sprinting back and starting to press again. At the same time, the team that just conceded can restart from their goalkeeper and attempt to get further up the field. However, the goalkeeper must play short to prevent it becoming a long pass to an unmarked player, which would be too easy. The quicker the defending team recovers, the higher and more aggressively they can press. Players will find themselves in unfamiliar positions due to the nature of the game. For example, a defender on the team that scored will get to their defensive line first and will then have to press as a forward, and vice versa for the forwards. Play 3x5 minute games and keep the score at all times.

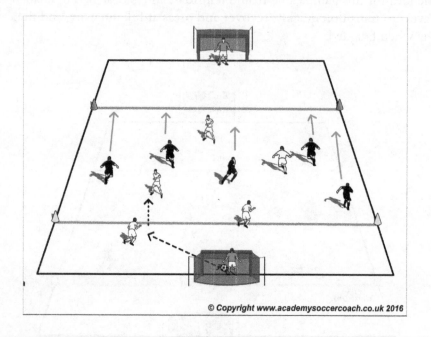

© Copyright www.academysoccercoach.co.uk 2016

Progressions:

- Make the field bigger and increase the distances from the defensive lines.

- Only three players have to hit the lines and recover. This means that for a certain period of time, a team will have to defend an overload so they will have to work extra hard to make up for lack of numbers.

- Remove the defensive line and make it the goal line where teams now have to recover before pressing. It might be a good idea to add a pass minimum here for the team in possession in order to give the recovering team time in which to get back and work.

Exercise Five

We have already discussed the importance of movement for games-based training, during the preseason period. It adds intensity and creates an environment where players have to perform under duress and fatigue. Another important factor which helps create these optimal conditions for preseason is competition. The focus on this exercise is to take advantage of the excitement that the players derive from 5v5 games and create a higher physical workload and overloads on both sides of the ball. Designed by Clifton Bush, assistant coach at Cal State Bakersfield, the game is set-up like a normal 6v6 game but with two differences. Firstly, the game must take place in the middle of the field, or with a big space around it. Secondly, there must be balls placed on top of cones around the perimeter.

Both teams can play a free-flowing competitive 6v6 game and there are no limitations on touches or team shape. There is, however, one condition. If a player misses the target with a shot on goal, or misplaces a pass outside the playing area, they must run and recover the same ball that they kicked out. The game is restarted by the opposition who can dribble any of the balls on top of the cones. The recovering player must replace a ball on top of one of the outside cones before they can re-enter the game. This game condition creates two scenarios. Firstly, the defensive team has lost a player for a short period of time and must adapt accordingly. Secondly, communication and workloads must be increased by the man-down team to overcome the disadvantage. The player who has to recover the ball must do so at full speed and will usually have to cover sprints of over 20 yards so they are more similar to physical demands of a game. To keep the intensity levels of the game as high as possible, play for four minute increments and replace the balls on the cones during the recovery.

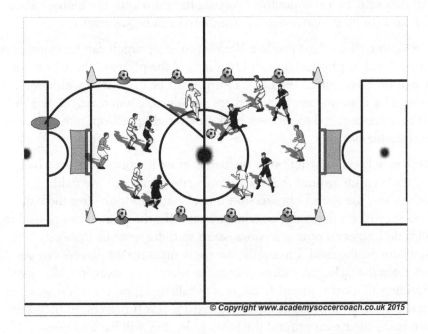

Technical Progressions:

- Before the recovering player re-enters the game, they must do a technical challenge. It can be a skill test like a certain number of juggles or toe taps that they must complete.
- If you have three teams playing, where one team recovers off the field, incorporate them for the skills challenge also. For example, before a player reenters the field they must beat a resting player in a 1v1 situation, or combine with that player for 20 successive headers.
- Before a team can score during an overload situation, every player on the team must touch the ball. This will create an urgency in their passing and increased movement to create angles and space.

Exercise Six

Previous exercises have been created to condition players to work at their maximum capacity through attack and defense phases of play. This exercise works on placing the same physical exertions during the possession phase, which is a time when tempo can sometimes drop to a comfortable level for both teams. This exercise also sets challenges for players and teams to taking up attacking positions, when in possession, that can hurt teams. Players who take shortcuts will find themselves on the periphery in an exercise like this and will not need a coach to tell them that. Likewise, as a competitive exercise, the team with the highest work ethic and ability to play when outnumbered will be successful.

A 6v6 game takes place inside a 30x50 yard area, which can be adjusted to suit the level or physical demand required of the players. Three poles are located on each side of the field. Teams must be organized with a set shape. This is important to hold them accountable when fatigue sets in and they are required to recover back to a certain position, rather than a comfortable one.

There is only one restriction in the game: after any player passes a ball, they must sprint around the nearest pole and back onto the field. Technically, the team in possession must be able to look after the ball when they face a defensive overload. Tactically, the player who passed the ball is no longer an option in possession so there must be options elsewhere on the field. Physically, the more quickly that players can get back onto the field, the more options the player in possession will have. Providing support is arguably the most challenging aspect of the game and smart work is just as important as the hard work. If players on the same team make their runs around the same pole, they will have to take different angles of support so will have to communicate that with each other.

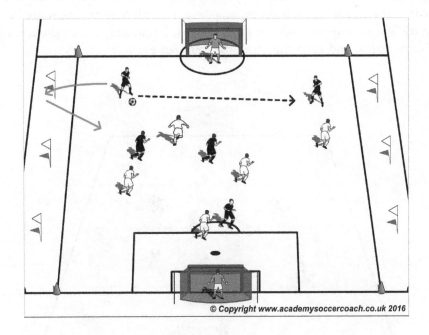

© Copyright www.academysoccercoach.co.uk 2016

Progressions:

- When a player gives the ball away, they must do the same thing as when a pass is completed and run around the pole before entering the game. You can add that to the current game restrictions or substitute them. The focus is now on the defensive end and you are looking for a positive reaction from a player who loses the ball.

Exercise Seven

Coaching inside the game is not just limited to the team in possession of the ball. Games can also be conditioned to reinforce defensive principles when players do not have the ball. Units and small groups are very important when team defending.

This exercise is a game which challenges players to press in a certain type of system. The first game (below) features twelve players who are split into two teams of six, including a goalkeeper on each team. The field is 60x30 yards in size and is divided into four zones, each 15 yards long. The scoring system is based around the defensive work of the team in black. When the white team is in possession of the ball, the black team must apply pressure and have five seconds to get their whole team inside two zones of the ball. When the team in possession progress the ball into a new zone, the zone rules change accordingly. If every player is not inside the two zones, the white team gets a point. The white team can score in the traditional way through the goal. Play for 5 minutes, switch the roles of both teams, and keep the score for four games.

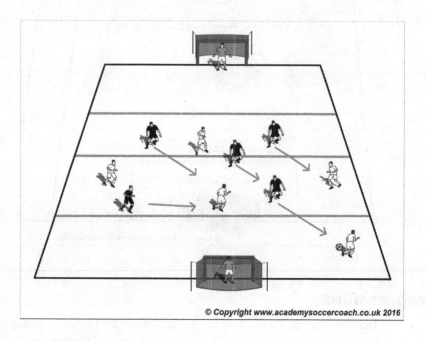

Progression:

- Time can be manipulated to put even more pressure on the team which presses.

- The game can be changed to a pressing game where compactness and keeping one team in one half of the field are the goals. There are five vertical channels on the field and, when the ball goes into a wide channel, all players on the defensive team, except one, must cover two channels within five seconds. If they win the ball in the wide zone, the defending team gets a point.

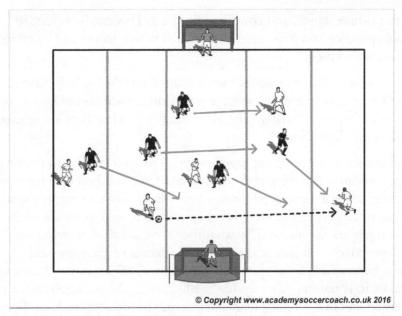

© Copyright www.academysoccercoach.co.uk 2016

Conclusion

When we are designing our preseason program, we must attempt to influence the mindset of the team and individuals with the same urgency that we want to impact their fitness levels. If traditional preseason training has programmed coaches to believe that our players will respond to just about any type of physical training, it may be time to seriously reconsider such a view. Yes, if you ask players to perform mind-numbing exercises unrelated to the game, they will do it, but the negatives may outweigh the positives. Boredom always kills focus.

Therefore, if you want a team to approach training with the right levels of motivation and focus, they must be provided with that *"why"* every day. Team culture is now at stake in the preseason stage. Applying games based training to your preseason program as soon as possible will immediately engage your players and give them a platform that they want to channel their energy and competitive drive into. Not only can these games provide a base for players to reach their physical maximum, but they also create opportunities to coach and challenge players in every facet of the game.

In his book *Soccer Tough*, sports psychologist Dan Abrahams talks about how the mindset of a player is largely driven by their movement and body language. Abrahams believes that "physiology changes psychology" and when players are moving quickly and without restraint, this freedom gives way to positive, quick, and confident thinking. This can be extended towards practice and preseason in particular where habits and behaviors are typically formed.

I'm also a big believer in a coach possessing the ability to help shape a player's mentality in a really positive way. Enthusiasm is contagious, and so is lack of it, unfortunately! Players work better when they are engaged and if we can help them.

If enthusiasm and energy are regular visitors to your preseason training camp, you can make some serious progress. Coaches therefore must work hard in creating a training program where players are moving, engaged, and can reach their optimum levels of focus. We must be aware of the fact that players are inspired by what they love, *not what the coaches love.* Although coaches dream of discussing the details of the game and debating everything from systems to set-piece routines, most players are bored by it. If training is enjoyable, it will sustain players when they are exhausted and this can take teams over many hurdles throughout the season.

6

Sustaining High Intensity

One definition of football fitness is that it's the ability of a team to function in the last minute of a match with the same quality and endeavor with which they began the game.

Sustaining performance levels in the modern game is getting more and more difficult and the number of late goals is on the rise. Of course, the physical side of the game plays a major role, but other areas have impacted this trend significantly.

Technically, as skill execution levels drop in the closing stages of games, more defensive mistakes are made and forwards are more than happy to capitalize. It is the equivalent of basketball's last second shot, where a forward finds himself in the 'right place at the right time' to become the hero and win the game. When Lionel Messi scored his 374th goal for Barcelona in 2015, remarkably 38% of them were from the 85th minute onwards. The Argentinian's ability to produce technical excellence in the latter stages of games is one of the reasons why he is among the greatest to ever play the game.

Tactically, teams have usually figured out a weakness in the opposition that they have spent the majority of the game searching for, and are now in a position to take advantage of it.

Mentally, the rise and rise of pressure has led to panic inside penalty boxes, and, combined with the drop in focus levels, both can cause teams to make mistakes that they would never have dreamt of making during the opening stages of a game.

The closing stages of a game *must therefore be a target area* for teams to focus on – during their preseason training.

The relationship between practice and performance is certainly not a new phenomenon. In 650 B.C. Greek soldier Archilochus announced, "We don't rise to the level of our expectations; we fall to the level of our training." In today's world of marginal gains, this connection must be stronger than ever before because our players are facing more complex physiological challenges than any previous generation. Pushing beyond limits in training almost creates a placebo for teams where they gain this incredible self-belief. The game itself almost feels easier than the training sessions and teams can finish strong because players believe they have earned the right to do so.

In his book *The Gold Mine Effect*, Rasmus Ankersen traveled to a number of high performance cultures to investigate what exactly takes athletes to the elite level. One of the 'gold mines' he visited was in Kenya to study their highly successful long distance runners. Ankersen met with professor of exercise and sports science Tim Noakes, who believes that it is not genetics, talent or ability, but instead the demands that the Kenyans impose on themselves during training that separates them from the rest of the world. "If you look at Kenyan runners, they have a different attitude to pain and they push intensity of training to a whole new level. When they start feeling discomfort, I don't think they see it as pain in the same way that others do. They see it as a challenge."

Can this theory transfer to soccer? I believe it already has. Many teams struggle to maintain a playing style for long periods of time because they have an inability to recover from bouts of high intensity work at a quick enough rate. This is directly impacted by their practice habits and the amount of physical, technical, tactical, and psychological stress players are exposed to regularly on the training pitch.

Of course, you cannot use stress, intensity and preseason in the same breath today without the topic of overtraining arising. With intense media attention on the game today, coaches of the best teams in the world get heavily criticized when players pick up injuries during the preseason period. Because of such negativity and criticism, the threat of overtraining has led to many coaches working in fear and placing a ceiling on the workload that they prescribe to their teams. Recent evidence has proved that this may not actually be the case, however.

Tim Gabbett, a highly-acclaimed, Australian sports scientist has been working in injury prevention and performance maximization for 20 years. His ground-breaking work has found that high workloads can actually reduce the risk of injury and that undertraining actually increases injury risk. Gabbett believes that too many teams are training for the average demands of the game, and this causes them to be underprepared for the most demanding passages of play. "We need load to develop resilience. We need load to get fit. We need load to compete at the very highest level.

Otherwise, the other extreme is we go into competitions under-prepared and then we get injured."

Gabbett is very much an advocate of 'train harder and smarter' and believes high loads can protect against injury, provided you get there safely. From a safety aspect, excessive and rapid increases can be responsible for non-contact, soft-tissue injuries. Players also have to understand that if they train hard, they must recover hard as well. Gabbett's work could lead to dramatic consequences for how coaches structure preseason training moving forward. The objective of preseason is not only to get our players working at a high intensity, it is keeping them there!

In this chapter we will look closely at how to take sessions to the next level so that our players can recover quickly during the game and sustain the desired playing style from start to finish.

What kills high intensity

Before adding anything to a training program, we must evaluate all aspects of the environment so that we are not simply adding for the sake of it. Bruce Lee called it "Hacking at the inessential". It is one thing to identify the importance of recovery and sustainability in the modern game, but it is another thing to improve it. Players are habitual and they practice how they play. Many aspects of traditional coaching make it difficult to implement and below are just a few of these.

Training inside the physical comfort zone – Exercises and sessions must be physically challenging enough to get all players towards their maximum energy expenditure. The 2v2 exercise below, where two attackers in white go against two attackers in black, is a prime example. The exercise takes place inside a 20x20 yard area, and the same attacking and defensive movements are being made over and over again. Players have been doing exercises like this since they started playing the game and, although it can be a good teaching tool for basic playing principles, the movement required on both sides of the ball are second nature by the time they reach a competitive level. As a result, the challenge level is normally too low for players to be pushed at their maximum both physically and technically.

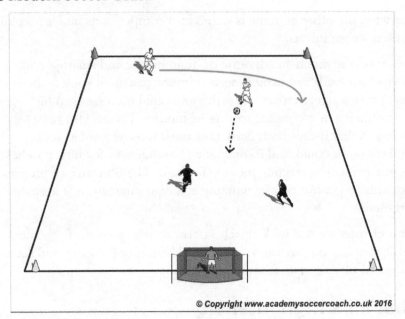

© Copyright www.academysoccercoach.co.uk 2016

Small playing areas – On a similar theme to type of exercise, if the size of the pitch is small, players will never be required to step outside their comfort zone in terms of movement and physical demands. There are too many natural recovery positions in small sided games where players can get rests without getting exposed.

Long lines – If players perform an action and then have to stand in line for long periods of time, the exercise can be counter-productive, no matter how challenging the action is. Coaches should also be aware of work-to-recovery ratios in every preseason activity. If a player is performing one high intensity action and then has a three-minute break, chances are their match fitness development curve will not be very steep.

Too much coaching – Although every coach has plenty of on-field work to do during the preseason period, there is a time and place to deliver it. Time, especially, is an important consideration and coaches will struggle to challenge players physically if they are sitting them down for long periods at a time for the benefit of tactical lectures. It can also break focus and Jurgen Klopp believes there is a link between the two. "Physical problems come when you get tired in the mind, then the body follows."

Endurance over intensity – Long distance runs and lengthy possession games are both becoming redundant in the modern game. A team cannot train at one intensity and expect to adopt another one during a game. In *The Modern Soccer Coach 2014*, we identified the three C's (clock, competition, and communication) as the drivers of tempo and intensity on the training pitch.

Exercise One

Recent studies have shown that the game is becoming more and more compact with less space on the field and time on the ball. Because of this, the number of explosive actions (sprints/duels, etc.) have increased by 40% over the last 8-10 years. This exercise exemplifies that trend and incorporates recovery within both build-up phase and attack versus defense. There is also an element of supporting runs, combination play, and a transitional aspect too. The tactical side of the game that we are looking to work on here is playing off a target forward and providing support as quickly as possible. Of course, the quality of hold-up play from the target forward is also a vital component of success, with movement to create space just as important as technique.

The exercise is set up inside a narrow playing field within both 18 yard boxes. Players are split into two teams. One target forward is set up against two defenders on both halves of the field. Play begins from the goalkeeper who plays out to one of the defenders in black. The defenders have split to create angles and upon receiving the first pass, the first defender then passes to the next. This is the cue for the target forward to accelerate towards the ball and receive an entry pass from the second defender.

As soon as the ball is played, both defenders in black now become midfielders and sprint up to provide support and join the target forward. A 3v2 is created towards goal. Once the attack ends, the exercise now works the other way with the goalkeeper playing one of the white defenders. Two new black defenders must then move into the appropriate positons while the players who supported the initial attack must work on their recovery back to where they began. At any stage, if the defenders win the ball, they can counter-attack immediately and the exercise continues. Players must recover back on the outside of the field and are not allowed to walk back to position.

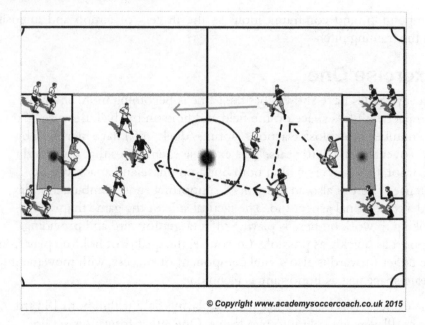

© Copyright www.academysoccercoach.co.uk 2015

Progressions:

- Add a time limit on the attack from the moment the goalkeeper starts with the ball. This will put pressure on the build-up and add urgency to the attack.
- Add a second ball to every attack so that players have another transitional moment to work on.
- Give the players on the recovery run a timed target in which to get back to their starting positions. This will not only challenge them physically but build good habits of getting back behind the ball as soon as possession is lost.

Exercise Two

Teams who can recover together as a unit are normally very difficult to break down when they do not have the ball. Once recovery becomes part of the team ethos, defenses become organized more quickly and even create opportunities to win the ball straight back after losing it.
Developing this shape and work rate with your team is the goal here with a multifunctional defensive exercise that Jurgen Klopp used during his time at Borussia Dortmund. It is an extremely thought-out exercise which combines basic shape and tactical principles with the chaos that can arise once overloads develop during a game. Klopp has prided his teams in

being extremely disciplined with phenomenal organization when out of possession and this could well be one of the reasons why.

The exercise takes place ten yards either side of the halfway line and involves the back four in black, and attacking players in white. The field is split into four areas across the field and each area is occupied by a defender with an attacker facing directly opposite. As they match up together, there are two additional attacking players on the outside sidelines. There will be a goalkeeper behind the four defenders on one side and a coach will act as a server behind the attackers on the other.

The exercise is broken down into two parts. The initial phase only involves the four defenders and the four adjacent attackers. The two wide attackers are not part of it. All players stay in their own area. The attacking players pass the ball square and each time the ball arrives at an attacker's feet, the defender directly opposite steps up to apply pressure. As the attacking player passes the ball square and the ball leaves the area, the same defender retreats to their original line. It is a simple exercise of pressure, shifting, and covering but also allows defenders to pick up cues such that they will be able to see the ball arriving by the body shape of the passer. This is a basic exercise that many teams apply and is important as players establish roles and responsibilities for shape across the back four.

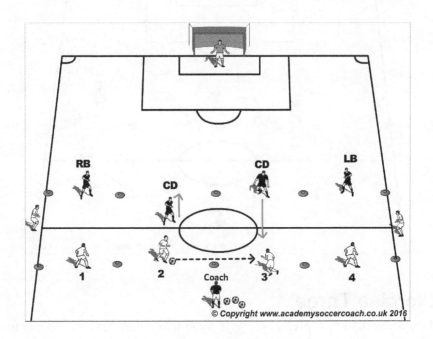

The Modern Soccer Coach

On the coach's signal, the exercise transitions into a 6v4 towards goal. The first ball is out of the exercise as soon as the coach triggers the second ball into one of the wide players, who then start the attack towards goal. The first role of the defenders is to retreat towards goal but also to stay balanced. The back four want to drop and stay compact, but they must be unwilling to drop into their own 18-yard box. This is a critical coaching point because once a back four drops into that area, they are unable to apply any pressure on the ball towards attacking players, as well as being vulnerable to crosses.

Defensive success relies so much on individuals working together as a group. If one person switches off, especially at the highest level, it will almost certainly result in a goal. Communication is vital but when this exercise is transferred to a game in a stadium packed with 80,000 people, everyone must be on the same wavelength. The discipline to establish roles and responsibilities must be done on the practice field at full speed. With the exercise being so realistic to the game, you can see that the success Dortmund and Klopp had, is certainly no coincidence.

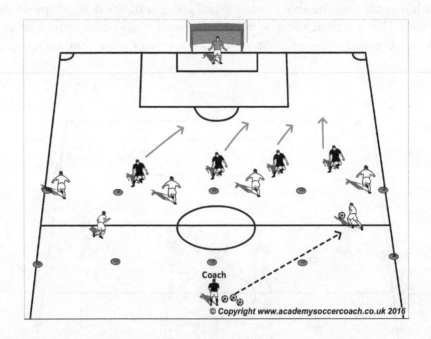

Coach

© Copyright www.academysoccercoach.co.uk 2016

Exercise Three

More often than not, players struggle most when they have to recover into defensive positions. Most attacking players are reluctant to get back into a defensive position when they lose possession of the ball and it can lead to many chances and goals at the other end. Back fours are often left exposed and teams have no choice but to drop and concede space. This exercise attempts to condition players to recover in two key areas: an initial transition to defensive duties, and then a transition back to offense.

Where the exercise is slightly different, however, is that the attacking transition is without doubt the more difficult of the two. If the players put the work in early, they will earn a rest with a recovery point at the halfway line. If they are slow with their recovery run, however, they will feel as if the running never stops.

The exercise takes place on one half of the field with three teams of five players each. There are also two forwards who play for the attacking team at all times. Prior to the exercise starting, players must have both an attacking and defensive position. This will be important for them, as they will be held accountable to these positions when fatigue sets in. The exercise begins with the black team (plus two forwards) attacking the white team in a 7v5 towards goal. They have 12 seconds to score. If the defensive team wins the ball, they must try to break out in possession and dribble through gates at 1, 2, or 3. Once the attack is finished, the attacking team transitions to the defensive role.

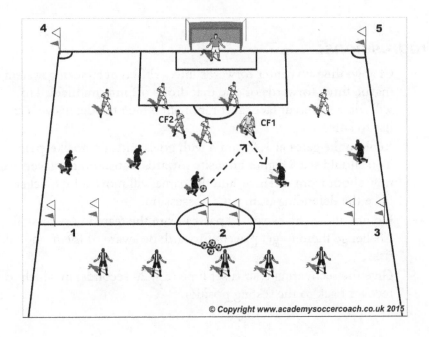

If the recovering team is not back behind the halfway line by the time the next attack is finished, they automatically lose a point. This is where team organization is important also. Wide players must re-enter at gates 1 or 3, while central players have extra work to do by having to arrive at gate 2.

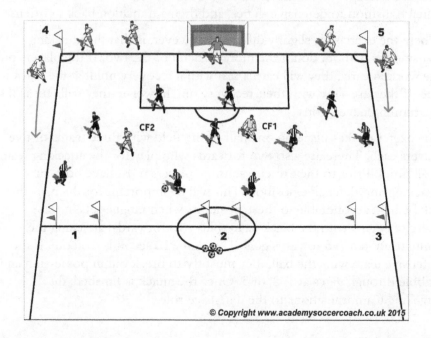

© Copyright www.academysoccercoach.co.uk 2015

Progressions:

- Change the two center forwards into a different attacking system – maybe three forwards or one that drops off into midfield. This will add a different tactical component which the defensive team has to solve.
- Replace the gates at 1, 2, and 3 with goals and add goalkeepers. You should see a higher intensity towards transition as players can now shoot from distance, and the game will move a lot quicker once the defending team wins possession.
- Do not allow any backward passes from the team in possession. Challenge them to get players forward, be aware of them, and take risks.
- Give the recovering team a set time (e.g. 20 seconds) in which to recover back to the resting position

Exercise Four

Many times we talk about recovery as something we have to do after an action on the field. For example, after an overlapping run and cross, the full back must recover into a defensive position. We must also be aware, however, that sometimes recovery happens *before* the actual action and is something that allows a player to perform key actions at critical times of the game. Forwards at the highest level sometimes talk about the importance of making two runs – one for the defender and one for them. The first run is designed to take the defender into a certain area (e.g. back post) and creates space for the second run to be made (front post) where they should have a clear run into space.

This is not only the function of attacking players. Dani Alves at Barcelona continually makes attacking runs without getting the ball and has to recover quickly when his team loses possession.

This exercise is designed for certain players to perform an explosive action before getting involved in defense or the attack. The competitive nature of the exercise also means that the team which does the physical work best, gives themselves an overload in a critical area of the field.

This is a 3v3 exercise with a difference. Attackers and defenders, along with a goalkeeper, are split into three groups on one half of the field. The attacking team is in white shirts while the defenders are wearing black. Play begins when the attacking player A1, plays a diagonal ball to A2 at the halfway line. As soon as the ball is played, D3 and A3 must sprint around the mannequins before they can join the move. When the ball arrives at A2, he/she can attack to goal and D2 can become a live defender. At the same time, A1 takes up a central forward positon and D1 takes up a central defensive position. Both pressure and options are coming from both directions and the team who recovers into position first will be in pole position. It can become a specific exercise where central defenders, fullbacks, defensive midfielders, attacking midfielders, wingers, and center forwards all get realistic practice in their own positions.

© Copyright www.academysoccercoach.co.uk 2016

Progressions:

- Add a run for both A1 and D2 so that they are challenged slightly more to take their initial positons. You will then see if A1 can become more effective if he/she takes D1 to another area of the field and creates space for A2 or A3.

- Give the defensive team a goal if they win the ball. A very simple one is to run with the ball beyond the halfway line, but you can add mini-goals or target players to challenge them to pass out and score.

- After the attack is finished, create a competition between the same group where all players must recover back to their initial positions. The first team that arrives back scores a point. It's a great way to emphasize another recovery run after the initial ones.

Exercise Five

Two of the first things to deteriorate when teams get tired are technical ability and organization. Technical ability is an individual casualty of fatigue, especially in preseason when the players are coming off a long layoff without the ball. Towards the end of a session, first touches are not always the cleanest and many passes can go astray. Organization is more of a team concept but you will always find spaces open up with tired teams because players do not recover to where they should be, and players do not problem solve quickly enough. Transition exercises can constantly test a team's ability to set-up and re-group effectively because the conditions of the game constantly change. This exercise works on both challenging individual players to maintain a high level of technical ability, and teams to constantly organize and re-organize under constant pressure. Sometimes teammates can get away with costing their team during tactical reorganizations, but small sided games highlight problem areas because one player missing can prove costly for defenses.

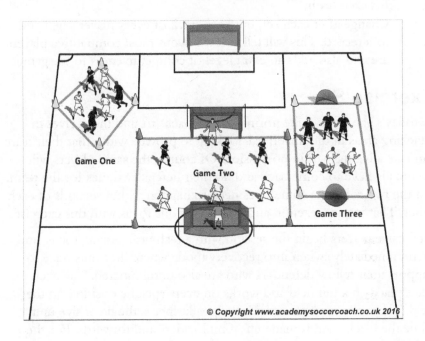

© Copyright www.academysoccercoach.co.uk 2016

Players are organized into teams of three. There are three different fields located on one half of the field. Field number one is a possession game played inside a diamond. This game is a 3v3 possession game where passing and angles of support play a major role in the success of a team. The rules are simple: five consecutive passes count as a goal.

Field number two is a 3v3 with full sized goals and goalkeepers.

Field number three is a 3v3 four goal game where teams are trying to find success in wide areas to score. The games last three minutes long and the challenge arrives on the transition. For the first set, the black team stays while the white team rotates from left to right. They have six seconds to rotate before the black team starts with the ball on their side of the field. If a team is slow to get to their field, play continues anyway. After two rotations, the teams take a two-minute break before switching roles. If possible, keep the score of every game and tally it up at the end. Make sure there is a good supply of balls around each field so that the game does not continually stop and players cannot take advantage of breaks.

Progressions:

- Add a running station in-between transitions for both teams. This will get them to a point of fatigue a lot quicker.
- Make the playing area bigger so that there is more ground to cover for each team.
- Change after each set, but keep track of every player's win and loss record. This will tell you who your most competitive players are and also adds an extra level of competitiveness to the game.

Exercise Six

In today's game it is quite normal for fullbacks to find themselves in attacking areas in the final third, looking to provide width that their team can take advantage of in possession. Of course, the same players will eventually have to have come back and do their defensive duties for the team, but the two roles can sometimes need to happen within seconds of each other. That instant reaction and recovery is our focus with this exercise.

Defensive players begin the session with a technical passing focus, and then immediately switch into recovery mode where they must race to support their fellow defenders who are also outnumbered. The exercise takes place on a full field and works on every specific position on the field. The white team along with the goalkeeper is the defensive unit, while the black team is made up of midfielders and forwards. For the defensive team, it is important to organize players into their set positions: D1 and D2 are fullbacks, D3 and D4 are center backs, and D5 is a holding midfielder.

The exercise begins with D5 who passes the ball to one of the fullbacks (D1 below). This first pass is a trigger for a number of movements on the other side of the field. The two center backs, D3 and D4, can come out and establish their initial defensive positions. Also, as soon as the first pass is made, D5 recovers into a defensive position. As D1 opens up in possession, he/she passes to the black central midfielder and must then recover immediately alongside D3 and D4. The central midfielder in black must play to the wide forward on the other side of the field and then the black team is free to attack goal in a 4v2 situation with two recovering white players (D1 and D5). After the attack ends, the next ball goes to D2 and the same pattern continues. The challenge for D1 is to try and recover into a position on the weak side and provide cover for the two center backs. If they do not get there quickly enough, the black team will have two wide options and should create an easy chance on goal.

Progressions:

- Allow both fullbacks (D1 and D2) to recover towards defensive positons at the same time. This will create a defensive overload and should create success for the black team.
- Provide the defensive team with a goal if they win possession. For example, if they dribble past the halfway line they score a point. This will increase the physical demands and competitiveness of the exercise.
- Add another forward player to the black team or another central midfielder. Then allow the black midfielder to pass to any player in the attack. This will challenge the white team to delay in their defending while help arrives on the recovery.

Exercise Seven

Defensive recovery is not just about defenders working to get back into defensive positions, it's also about them actually dealing with the attack effectively. So many late goals are a result of defenders who have done the work tactically with shape and discipline, but cannot technically execute what they need to, in the dying stages of the game. It might be a half clearance, a header directly to an oncoming attacking player on the edge of the box, or a sliced clearance that results in an unwanted corner. The goal of the defensive unit must therefore be not only to position themselves correctly on their recovery, but also to deal effectively with the attack so that their opponents cannot find a way through. This exercise may not be as physically demanding in terms of high-intensity runs, but it puts an enormous strain on the defensive unit and requires them to continually recover in terms of technique, as well as physical work.

This exercise takes place on one half of the field and involves a back four (in black below) and a goalkeeper, against three attackers and five servers positioned around the field approximately 30 yards from goal. These servers are numbered 1-5 and all players must be aware of which one is which. The coach starts the exercise by shouting a number and the server is free to play and join in the attack. When the server joins in the attack, they create a 4v4 to goal. After the attack ends, the coach gives the defenders six seconds to get outside their 18-yard box and then defend the next ball. Every server gets to play 3 balls so the back four has to defend 15 balls in total. For the defenders to score a point, they must clear the ball over the head of the line of servers. If the ball is too low, the servers can keep the ball in play and the attack continues.

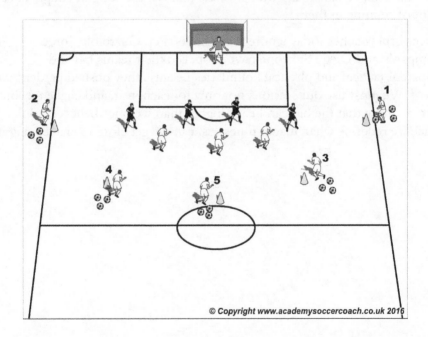

© Copyright www.academysoccercoach.co.uk 2016

Progressions:

- Allow the defenders 8 seconds to recover but they must hit the goal line after every attack ends. This means that the next attack will most likely take place as the defenders are just getting out of their own penalty box and it is a lot more physically demanding.

- Once their number is called, servers can drive forward with as many touches as they like and even score goals. This will put more pressure on the defense to step and remain compact.

Conclusion

Calling teams who score late goals 'lucky' creates excuses for players and takes away the focus and commitment required to become a great team. We may be led to believe that preseason is all about fitness work, but the real barrier to high performance is closer to mental than it is physical. Before Roger Bannister became the first man to break the four-minute mile, in 1965, most people thought it was impossible. The human body apparently was not built to be put through that kind of physical stress. However, two years later – 37 runners had achieved the same feat as Bannister. The same principles apply to soccer. Coaches are unintentionally imposing limits on their teams by the way they train. They are confusing 'challenging' with sessions that last too long or simply have a lot of running in them.

Successful coaches today ignore those limits. Pep Guardiola, Jorge Sampaoli, and Diego Simeone have propelled their teams beyond apparent tactical and physical boundaries because they pushed harder than most. We must use our sessions not only to teach, test, and challenge, but also to show that the bar can be set higher than we once believed. Only once we redefine what 'match fitness' is, can we get close to challenging it.

7

Possession

In this book, we have discussed many changes that have and are currently taking place between old school and modern day preseason models. Possession is one area which, again, is not a new concept by any means, but certainly one in which the evolution of the game has demanded that we re-evaluate how it is both taught and applied to training.

I have witnessed this evolution first hand in my development as a coach. During my first coaching course, possession and passing both went hand-in-hand under the same module. The coaching points included receiving the ball with different surfaces and the exercises were all performed in isolation, where passing was almost treated as a closed skill. You received the ball, adjusted your feet, took your touch, and then performed the exact same pass back to your partner. Right foot, then left foot – always on your toes so that the service didn't take you by surprise. Of course, a technical base is a requirement for young players before they can do anything else, but this was a course directed towards advanced players.

Under this school of coaching, passing exercises were largely successful because they were accurate and slow. This is not a criticism of the instructor or the course curriculum, but rather an indicator as to how the game has changed over the past 15 years. Traditional training was about control first, pass second, and everything was centered around straight lines with continuous repetition. In essence, it was a slow way of training to play what was then a slow game. Below is an example of how it was organized into a session. Nice straight lines, with the balls going back and forth, almost like a tennis practice. If you have been involved in coaching for over ten years, this probably looks somewhat familiar.

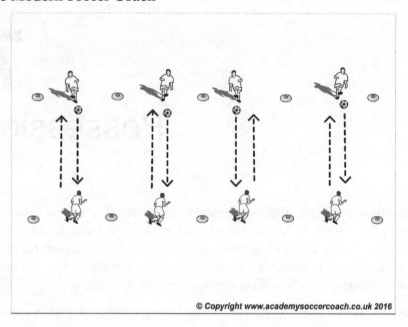

Today however, the possession aspect of the game has evolved to a whole new level where isolated passing exercises no longer match the demands of the game. Players today rarely receive the ball in straight lines, standing still, or facing each other. The technical, physical, tactical, and mental components of the game are all interdependent. Spanish legend Xavi is a believer that the ability to make quick decisions is more important than anything else. "The speed at which you think is more important than your physical speed."

Not only is the game quicker today, but modern coaches are being influenced by new research and imagination that has stretched minds as we aim to bring training as close as we can to the game itself.

Wolfgang Schollhorn, a professor from Mainz University and human movement specialist, developed the method of differential practice where he emphasizes variety and fluctuation as key components of the learning process. Instead of aesthetically-pleasing exercises like straight lines for example, he believes that mistakes are necessary for players to develop 'self-organizing processes', whereby they can react to the many different situations that will arise during a game.

Along similar lines, Michel Bruyninckx, a coach with the Belgian FA and one of the most forward-thinking coaches in recent years, believes that brain-centered training is the key to technical training at all ages. "You have to present new activities that players are not used to doing. If you repeat exercises too much, the brain thinks it knows the answers." Like Wolfgang Schollbern, Michel Bruyninckx believes in variable repetitions and many of his sessions focus on players having to double-task, along with rhythm, timing, spacing, and sometimes even synchronizations.

Below is an example of a basic Michel Bruyninckx exercise. The player on the ball can pass to the left or right side and must then move in the opposite direction to which they passed the ball. Players without the ball must react accordingly and rotate into the space vacated by the player in front of them. The shape of the exercise is a diamond, which is more realistic to modern playing systems than straight lines.

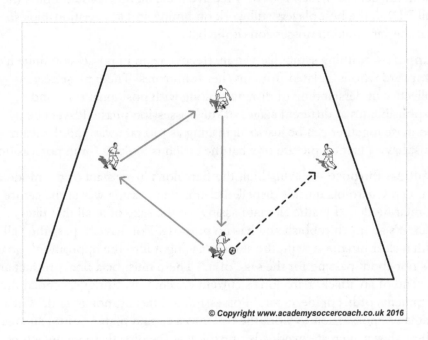

Preseason Possession Principles

Preseason is not about introducing the most complex passing exercises that you can find. The genius of Bruyninckx's work is that simplicity and complexity are never too far away, and there is always a strong relationship with the actual demands of the game. Our preseason possession exercises will incorporate the following principles:

Movement – Marcelo Bielsa credited this as one of the most important values of the game, not just possession. "Football for me is movement. You always have to be running. In football there are no circumstances for a player to stand still on the pitch." Players should never be static during possession exercises. They need to understand how to facilitate the use of space and what the 'triggers' are for specific tactical movements during a game. Cones are used as reference points for players to start at, not as positions where they stand and wait for the ball to arrive.

Angles – The higher the level, the more critical that subtleties in possession become. One yard, or the correct body shape, can be the difference between a player having the opportunity to play a killer pass or having to go 20 yards back to a teammate. Borussia Dortmund defender Nevan Subotic attributes the small details to the success of his team. "Under Thomas Tuchel we learn a lot about ball possession. It is really about the details. Which foot do I receive the ball; how should I pass the ball." Even the best players still work on timing and key relationships so that they are fluid in possession of the ball.

Support – Nothing symbolises an ineffective team in possession quite like a forward who is isolated from his/her teammates. There must be a collective understanding of distances along with positional roles and responsibilities at different stages of the possession phase. Players being too close together can be just as damaging as too far away and the team must have a tactical picture of what the coach is looking for in possession.

Tactical Purpose – Having built the Barcelona juggernaut of the modern era, Pep Guardiola quickly dispelled claims that passing was at the centre of their model. "I loathe all that passing for the sake of it, all that tika-taka. It's so much rubbish and has no purpose. You have to pass the ball with a clear intention, with the aim of making it into the opposition's goal. It's not about passing for the sake of it." There must be a final product at the end of an attack. Barcelona's current coach, Luis Enrique, echoed the comments of his predecessor, "Possession is a means, not an end." Great teams use possession to work the ball into a certain player or into an area where they can create overloads or exploit space directly to manufacture an opportunity on goal.

Speed and Quality – There is often a negative correlation between tempo and quality when you step outside the elite level of the game. If the intensity level of a session increases, the technical quality of the passing sometimes does the exact opposite. Players rush decisions and passes can go astray. However, part of developing teams and improving players is to make sure both increase simultaneously. Therefore, the goal of modern possession exercises should be to challenge players to think as quickly as they move and – at the same time – to produce a high level of technical execution.

Playing Forward – Although patience is a key quality of possession, when players sense an opportunity to penetrate defensive lines, often through congested areas around the opposition's penalty area, they must take advantage. Against good teams, the window of opportunity does not stay open for long, so players must be able to recognize such moments and possess the technical ability to exploit them.

Fighting Fatigue – Players are always comfortable in possession at the start of a training session or game. Fatigue impairs technical ability, and decision making, and makes it difficult for players to provide support effectively. Players must therefore be prepared and equipped to deal with those problems. Unless coaches proactively drill for imperfect conditions in training, they will surface under the pressure of competition.

Types of Preseason Possession Exercises

Although technique must be a focal point in possession exercises, it should not be the sole objective. As coaches, we must look beyond the simple passing exercises and try to extract more from our players. Below are three types of possession exercises that we will focus on during preseason.

Positional – This is where coaches can work in direct relation with their playing model. Set playing patterns are first established and then developed to a level which can create space or attacking platforms for a team to exploit. These patterns can aid, accelerate, or remove the thought process for players in possession. They also act as a blueprint for how a team can build in possession and pass the ball. This helps a team play together because positional play establishes movement patterns as well as passing ones.

Transitional – Possession exercises should not simply be focused around what a team does when they have the ball, they must also provide collective reactions, cues, and movement patterns once the ball is lost. Brendan Rodgers identified this as a key area throughout his time at Swansea and Liverpool. "You'll see in some of our exercises, a lot of our work is around transition and getting the ball back very quickly. Because I believe if you give a bad player time, he can play. If you give a good player time, he can kill you." Transitional exercises typically have a high physical demand as well as the requirement for players to make quick decisions under pressure.

Penetration – These exercises take place inside the final third and are characterized by opposed training, 'killer passes', and dynamic movements ahead of the ball. Without the 'killer pass', forwards will become frustrated and teams will be starved of goalscoring opportunities. These exercises are not set patterns, but instead must be varying repetitions that challenge players to possess a level of tactical creativity and test their technique in high pressure situations. Former AC Milan and Real Madrid playmaker Kaka identified three components of penetrating passes. 1. See the opportunity for the pass. 2. Chose the right moment. 3. Put the right weight on the pass.

Exercise One

Exercises that focus on patterns can come in a variety of shapes and forms. The challenge that arises at preseason is how to add a physical element to this in order to enhance fitness levels or challenge individuals to play quickly. Without opposition, players can sometimes set their own speed for technical exercises and it can often become too easy and unrealistic if you transferred that tempo to the game. However, if we know that technique can break under both pressure and fatigue, we want to try and expose our players to that challenge point during these exercises. Both exercises have similar forms of organization and focus on attacking play from the midfield into the final third. Focus, during the exercise, is therefore placed on dynamic movements. Both pattern exercises we will use are for 4-4-2 shapes but coaches can alter starting points or combinations to suit their system or playing model.

The first exercise, below, involves a team working a pattern down one side of the pitch. Players are split into two groups and organized in two similar shapes. The coach is the server and triggers the beginning of the exercise with a pass to the fullback. As soon as the fullback receives the ball, the center forward moves off the mannequin. This is the same movement pattern for all players – they must move off their mannequin when the ball is on the way to the player... one pass before they receive it. This way, they will be on their toes, arriving towards the ball and it will speed up the exercise. The full back plays to the center forward, who lays it off to the center midfielder, who then plays it wide to the winger. The center forward and center midfielder must get in the box and the winger will deliver a cross. The same pattern then takes place on the other side with the black team, as the white team recovers to their starting positions. After ten sets, both teams switch sides.

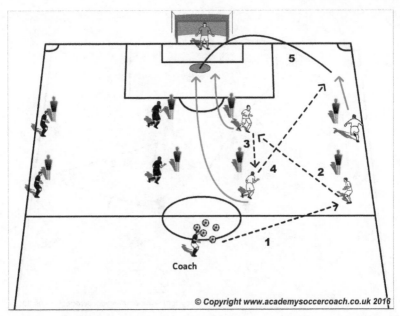

© Copyright www.academysoccercoach.co.uk 2016

The second exercise now focuses on patterns involving a full team using the full width of the pitch. One team performs the pattern while the other team recovers. The black midfielders play the ball wide to the winger, who drives inside and passes to the center forward. Similar to the first exercise, the coach must identify the moment for players to come off the mannequins and check to the ball. The second midfielder then receives the ball and switches the play to the oncoming left winger, who then delivers a cross. The physical challenge here arrives in two forms. Firstly, all players are required to get in the box for the cross. Secondly, after the pattern, the team must sprint behind the goal and then around the pitch and back to their starting point before the next rotation.

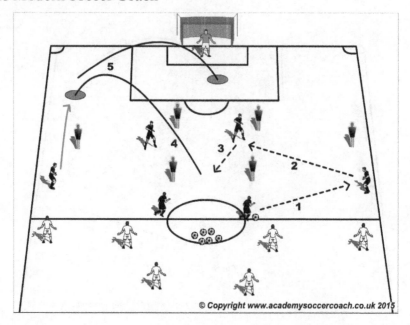

© Copyright www.academysoccercoach.co.uk 2015

Exercise Two

Although the quality of passing at most levels of the game has improved significantly over the past ten years, I personally feel that the pass after a dribble is becoming a lost art. Barcelona is quite rightly praised as a phenomenal team in possession but when you watch them play, they are masters of both passing and penetration. Almost every player, including central defenders, can drive into spaces with the ball and then find a pass. Messi is, obviously, outstanding at it.

It is the ability to move at full speed, choose the best option, and then put both the correct weight and angle on the pass that make it such a difficult aspect of the game . The closer to goal you get, the more complex the variables of time and space seem to become. Teammates also become reliant on one another to either move into or out of space. Everything must be performed at full speed, which also puts an emphasis on technique and timing.

This exercise focuses on attacking at speed, combination play, and adding a 'killer pass' to the possession phase. Timing is such an important factor here with players checking into the ball and then making runs beyond each other. Players start at four cones and work in pairs to combine with target forwards. There are two target forwards, who simply rotate with one another after each move finishes. Player A starts the exercise by driving towards the bottom goal. At the same time, the first target forward checks towards the ball and Player B advances their position up the field. As soon as the target forward checks into the ball, Player A lifts his/her head and Player B sprints in to create an angle for the pass. The target player lays the ball off at an angle to Player B, who then plays a first time pass into space for Player A to run onto and finish on goal. Player B continues their run and is on hand for any rebounds. Players A and B finish and recover behind the goal, the target forwards switch and the exercise then moves in the other direction with Players C and D.

The second stage of the exercise starts with the same initial passing pattern and movement. The difference is the type of run player A makes and the type of pass they receive from Player B. We are now looking for more width in the run and pass which sends Player A a little wider. The target forward also spins off after the pass and gets in the box for a cross. Player B also arrives into the box late for rebounds or a cross that is pulled back.

Progression:

- Add defensive players to the exercise, who can be passive for the
  initial pass and then fully active for the second.

Exercise Three

We have all marvelled at the keep ball exercises, or *rondos* as they are
known, by Barcelona and Bayern Munich. It feels like every week there is
a new Bayern one posted on YouTube where the ball zips about at full
speed and the players in the middle almost seem dizzy, without even the
slightest opportunity of winning the ball back.

I believe that these exercises are excellent for testing technique, working
on passing angles, and including a competitive element which makes them
popular with elite players in every culture. However, as coaches we have
to be careful where we place these exercises in our program as they
sometimes encourage bad habits that you don't want your team to
develop during preseason. Often, players have an opportunity to stand
around and quality levels can drop as quickly as heart rates do.

The following two exercises are progressions of traditional rondo
exercises in two ways. Firstly, we introduce a physical component that
challenges players to either recover or press at their maximum speed.

Secondly, we add an accountability factor where players are under pressure to keep possession as it will have consequences for their team.

This first exercise adds the physical component to rondos and challenges players to compete against one another. Players are organized into groups of five in 10x10 yard squares. It is a good idea to group players by similar levels of athletic ability. Each group has three poles placed 10, 20, and 30 yards away. Play begins as a normal 4v1 rondo with each player limited to one or two touches, depending on the ability of the group. On the coach's signal, the rondo stops and all players must sprint around the first pole and back. The last player to arrive back into the grid now becomes the defender in the new 4v1. This incentivizes the physical work that the players must do and also adds a competitive element to it. On the second call, the players must sprint to the second marker, and so on, before then working their way back down so that they do six sprints in total before a recovery.

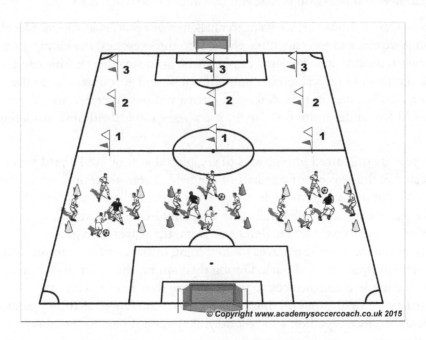

© Copyright www.academysoccercoach.co.uk 2015

Progressions:

- Instead of following the '1-2-3' pattern, the coach now calls out a number randomly and the players must react quickly to it. This tests players' focus levels, in addition to their speed.

- If the players restart the rondo and give possession away within ten seconds, the group must go again and redo the run. This progression seeks to maintain possession quality control and hold players accountable for giving the ball away cheaply if they are tired.
- Change the distances of the poles and the movement patterns. For example, backwards or sideways. This can increase the physical challenge or be incorporated in the dynamic warm-up.

Exercise Four

Another habit that you want to develop in preseason is collective awareness in the value of keeping possession. As I mentioned in the last exercise, rondos are not designed to put any great deal of responsibility on players' shoulders if they give the ball away. The atmosphere is typically relaxed with a bit of fun attached to it, and the biggest consequence of squandering possession is that you become the new defender.

In preseason, however, we want to challenge our players at a higher level, and if we can add a competitive element to the exercises, the connection between rondos and the game can be made even stronger. In this exercise, we aim to add physical work, competitiveness and accountability to the exercises. Because of this, defensive intensity should increase and players should feel under more pressure to use possession instead of squandering it.

Players are organized into groups of six, placed in four 10x10 yard grids, located in the corners of one half of the field. There are four poles in the middle, located approximately 15-20 yards from each grid respectively. The game starts as a 4v2 rondo with two randomly selected defenders. Once the ball is won by the defensive team, the player who gave possession away *and* the player to their right, must sprint around the pole nearest to their grid and back. During their sprint, the other players must try to complete 25 consecutive passes before they return, with two restrictions: firstly, they all must be on the outside line so that they cannot stand too close together; and secondly, they cannot pass to the same person twice (another easy way of getting consecutive passes).

If the running players return to the grid before the 25 consecutive passes are complete, the exercise continues. However, if the running players do not make it back in time, they have to go again until they do make it back in time. This should add a sense of urgency to both the physical work and a good tempo to the technical work inside the grid. Reactions must also be quick by the player who gave the ball away and the closest player to the right. If they delay their run, they will find it difficult to make it back in time.

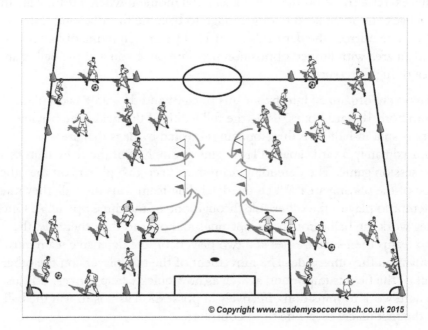

Progressions:

- Allow the group to step outside the grid and then decrease the number of passes the group must target. These passes can now be longer because the distances are bigger.
- Challenge groups to compete against each other. The first pair back gets two points and the first team to ten points win. The winning team can then pick a consequence (within reason) for the losing team to perform.

Exercise Five

Attacking transition is a crucial element of the game model. A team cannot simply counter every time they win the ball back so they must be able to shift from defense to attack by keeping possession of the ball. There is nothing more demoralizing for a defending team than to press like a hungry pack of wolves, only to give possession away almost as soon as they win it. On top of the frustration that it leads to, it also means that teams have to recommit to the hard work of winning the ball back again. Most players find this difficult because everyone would rather play with

The Modern Soccer Coach

the ball than without it. As a result, energy levels get depleted and spaces invariably open up.

This exercise focus on that key transitional moment when a team wins the ball back and must keep it long enough to become the attacking team. The game mirrors the demands of an 11v11 game, in terms of having to find an area with limited opposition pressure once you win the ball in an area of high pressure.

Players are organized into two teams of eight and the game takes place from both 18-yard boxes, using the full width of the field. The playing area is split in half with three openings created by flags that are approximately 3 yards apart. Play begins in one half of the field in an 8v6 possession game. The defending team must keep two players on the other side of the playing area. When the defending team wins the ball, they must attempt to play to the other side through one of the three openings. Once they work the ball through the openings and over to the other side, the two teams then switch roles and two players on the defensive team must remain on the other side. The movement of the two players on the other half of the field is important, as well as how quickly help arrives. It is just as hard work to transition effectively in possession as it is to win the ball in the first place; everyone must contribute.

© Copyright www.academysoccercoach.co.uk 2016

Progressions:

- Add a goalkeeper in each goal. If the team in possession gets eight consecutive passes, they can break out and go to either goal. Two attacking players are allowed to go and one defensive player can drop back.
- When the defensive team wins the ball in the 8v6, they must complete three passes before they can switch the play to the two players on the other side. This adds an even bigger challenge to the transition and will test players to keep possession while having to find a solution.

Exercise Six

As much as we all enjoy watching possession teams and "playing the right way", successful teams are actually the ones who can hurt the opposition in possession. They can move the ball quickly, create space, take risks, capitalize on opportunities, and make the correct decisions under pressure.

Being comfortable in passing the ball forward is one of the most underestimated aspects of possession. Most players can play backwards because there is no risk associated with it and you will rarely be criticized – but you will also never make a difference to a game. This is a multi-functional passing exercise that incorporates the technical, tactical, mental and physical aspects of possession football. Players are challenged to receive with an open body shape, create space for one another against a compact defensive block, and make quick decisions whether to retain possession or play forward. At the same time, there is a physical element to the exercise which allows players to be tested under fatigue and work conditioning under a competitive environment.

Players are organized into three teams with three players on each team. Two teams face each other in a 10x15 yard grid with three mini-goals. The third team starts at the halfway line with each player on a cone. The possession game of 3v3 is played by two teams who are restricted to their own half of the field. The objective is to move the ball from side to side in order to create space. The opposition are allowed to press up until the middle line. Once a space opens up, the team in possession aims to pass into one of the goals. If the opposition intercepts, they attempt to do the same. The only restrictions are that the players are limited to two touches (works on speed of play), teams are not allowed more than five passes before attempting to score (encourages penetration), and the ball must be below knee-height for a goal to count (technical quality of the pass must be high). The time of the game is determined by the third team, who must sprint from the halfway line to the goal line and back three times.

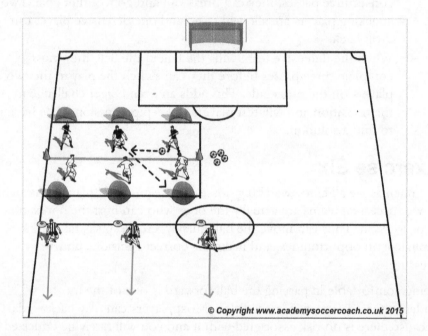

Progressions:

- One player in the defensive team can step beyond the halfway line and press the play. This will increase the speed of play and increase the physical demands of the game.
- Add conditions to the running team. For example, they must run backwards from the goal line to the halfway line. The more physically demanding the work for the third team, the greater the challenges will be when they must focus on possession with tired legs after they rotate.
- Increase the size of the 3v3 game and remove the middle line so that players are free to press and move in possession too. The tempo of the game should be high and players should still be encouraged to play forward when a space opens up.

Exercise Seven

As we addressed earlier, many possession exercises are set up to dictate to players *where* to pass and *where* to move afterwards. Everything is choreographed and the decision making process can inadvertently be removed completely. This is an exercise very much in contrast to that philosophy. It is a 5v2 rondo turned 8v8 game with a real competitive edge to it. The aim of the exercise is to combine the technical challenges of a rondo with the intensity of a game. There will be many mistakes and fatigue will play a role in a lot of them towards the end, but it will challenge the players in a variety of different ways, as well as indicating which players on your team are comfortable in possession of the ball in both tight and big spaces.

Players are organized into two teams of seven with a goalkeeper on each team. The game starts as a regular 8v8 game with no restrictions for 3 minutes. This time will give the players enough time to get their heart rates up and allow the game to develop a good tempo. At the 3-minute mark, the coach signals and each team must go back into their allocated 10x10 yard grid. The white team's grid is located in the upper left corner and the black team is located in the bottom right corner. Two defensive players from each team must go to the opposite corners and work as defenders. Once the players sprint into their grids, they now have 90 seconds to do a 5v2 rondo exercise. For every six consecutive passes, the team in possession earn a point. After 90 seconds, the players must transition again to the 8v8 match where they play again for three-minutes. The score from the rondos is continually added to the 8v8 game and after 4 sets, you will have a winning team. The defensive players must continually be rotated in the rondos so that every player has the opportunity to press and attempt to regain the ball. The possession team should be organized with four players on the outside and one player in the middle. The middle player must create angles and try to open up in possession.

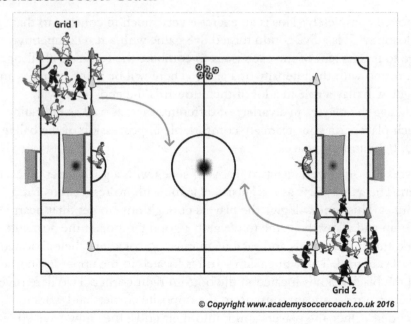

Progressions:

- Reward the possession aspect in the 8v8 game by awarding a goal for five passes inside the opponent's half. This will keep the tempo of the game as high as possible, which is important once fatigue is introduced.

- Give the possession team, inside the 5v2, six balls to play instead of a 90 second time limit. This will challenge them to make the most of possession and not be wasteful.

- Change the size of the possession grids or the conditions of the team in possession. You can limit their touch or make the area smaller so that the technical demands of the exercise increase as time progresses.

- Vary the conditions of the 8v8 game so that one team is in possession at all times (creating a 9v7 with the two goalkeepers), while the other team must win the ball back and can score on either goal.

Conclusion

Although possession was something of a novelty many years ago, it is definitely not the case anymore. The game is now full of players who are comfortable with the ball at their feet and who get impatient when passing choices are limited. Even to be a goalkeeper today, you must have outstanding technical ability and a range of passing that was once the prerequisite for a central midfielder.

Nowadays, the argument amongst coaches is how much possession is too much possession. Is there a purpose with the passing or are they doing it for possession's sake? Under Louis van Gaal, Manchester United have almost used possession as a form of defending. A slow build-up with players occupying fixed positions means that they are harder to break down in transition and defenders will rarely be in isolated positions. To be successful today, teams must be able to penetrate in the possession phase. Crowds no longer yell "ole" after twenty passes like they did many years ago, and instead want progress.

There must be a final product and teams like Barcelona and Bayern Munich have turned that balance of 'possession with penetration' into an art form. They use possession to draw the opposition out or draw players into positions they can benefit from. And they are ruthless when the chance arises. It takes tactical understanding, players who are prepared to make deliberate, forward runs into attacking areas, and of course, playmakers who have the technical ability to unlock the opposition. It is also difficult and takes a lot of work and commitment! It will take time to establish and improve key relationships so that everyone is clear about each other's roles. This is what preseason is for and coaches cannot afford to waste it.

8

Sometimes It Takes More

As coaches, not only do we spend our summer months in excitement and anticipation for preseason, we also tend to spend a lot of it in hope. The majority of coaches believe that a successful preseason hinges on their players reporting back on the first day with the highest levels of fitness possible. Is it too much to ask? In theory, it's probably not.

Most committed players will follow an individual summer conditioning plan, work with a personal trainer, or even train consistently with a summer or national team, so the chances are that they will come back in great shape. In addition, coaches always make an extra effort, before and throughout the off-season, to communicate the importance of high fitness levels and warn players that they must report back in the best condition possible.

Unfortunately for coaches, however, we don't live in an ideal world and perfect conditions rarely exist at any stage of the season, never mind the beginning of it. It seems that, even though every player in every team understands its importance, at least one or two players will come into preseason below general fitness requirements. It can even happen to the biggest and best teams in the world. In July 2014, after joining Manchester United for over $35 million, Luke Shaw was greeted with criticism of his physical condition by his new boss, Louis van Gaal who was so annoyed that he informed the world's media, "Luke needs to be fit and he's not very fit. He can't perform how I want." It may therefore be a little naïve for coaches to think that every player is going to report back in full fitness. Instead, we might be better off learning how to prepare for it when it actually does happen.

There is no easy answer here for coaches and certainly no quick fix. If you put extra load on the player in addition to their work with the team, you risk 'too much, too soon' and injuring the athlete. If you decide to banish the player away from training until they get their fitness levels up to the required level, you risk setting your team back. Missing team training sessions will lead to a player falling further behind physically, not to mention the important tactical and technical work that the player will forego. Alternatively, if you decide to do nothing and let the player work their way back into consideration by doing the regular training load, you risk damaging your team culture. Players who did the required work throughout the summer will feel aggrieved that they put in the hard yards when there was no consequence for not doing so. It could fracture team chemistry or lead your best trainers to question doing the work in the future. Either way, the team loses out. With so much at stake, this is surely where coaches need as much help and guidance as possible so that we can find the best solution for our teams.

Common Coaching Mistakes

With so many advances in sports science and constant changes in the game, coaches would be (like our unfit players above) guilty of poor preparation. They need to apply the correct level of knowledge and current understanding towards finding the best possible solutions. It is impossible to even attempt to manage the physiological requirements of our players without seeking advice and guidance from professionals who specialize in this area. Below are insights from sport science professionals from around the world on the biggest mistakes that coaches are making when faced with an unfit player reporting for preseason.

Too Much Too Soon – Even though coaches are aware of the problem, they still expect unfit players to handle the same high loads as every fit player, which leads them to injury, through overload and fatigue. Garga Caserta, Strength and Conditioning Coach of Portland Thorns FC, believes that this almost certainly results in a bigger problem for coaches down the road. "The number one factor for increased injury potential is an abnormal increase in physical load, and that is exactly what the coach will do by expecting the player who has not been practicing, to begin practicing at a high load in a new competitive environment."

Neglecting Strength Preparation – David Tenney, Sports Science and Performance Manager at Seattle Sounders FC, believes that strength training plays a key role in players who get hurt during preseason while trying to catch up to the group. "I think players who strength train well will not experience soreness as much, and may be able to turn over muscle fiber faster as they've been doing it all off-season. I also think there are some neural adaptations taking place that keep the body efficient in running."

The Modern Soccer Coach

One Size Does Not Fit All – Grouping all the unfit players together and expecting them to make the same progress does not work either. Tony Strudwick, Performance Coach at Manchester United, feels that coaches should manage individuals independently from the team. "The key is to individualize their program so that they do not breakdown, but still do enough to make progress with the group. You then must apply the principles of periodization and progression, and then ensure each individual is tracked, tested, and stretched appropriately."

Missing The Big Picture – Nathan Winder, Head of Sports Science at Barnsley Football Club, urges us to take a step back and look deeper when it comes to a player reporting into preseason in poor condition. "There may be a reason why they haven't returned in shape. The soft skills of the job are crucial in this area." Dealing with the situation without an understanding of the player's personal circumstances can lead a bad situation to become much worse, with a further decline in the player-coach relationship. On the flip side, if the coach can show empathy and understanding, the player may recommit themselves to the training and eventually get back to their best.

Mismanage Time – Michael Watts, Head of Sports Science at Aston Villa, believes that many coaches fail to fully understand the effects of fatigue and this can lead to them trying to speed the process up by ignoring their initial schedule. "Stick to the plan and make sure the player isn't overworked. When a player is fatigued they find it difficult to train at an intensity, which is what really makes the vital fitness gains. Fatigue also leads to injury." Michael believes that coaches also get the balance wrong between work and rest which can cause harm to players. "Days off and time to recover are vital. Work + Rest = Adaption but Work + Work = Fatigue. Often coaches won't give players time off as they think it will get them fitter."

Misread Demands – Nathan Gardiner, Tottenham Hotspur's Fitness Coach, believes that during pre-season training must be adapted to meet the requirements of the game and, therefore, exercises need to be as specific to the game as possible. "A big mistake that players normally make is that they work for big durations at a steady-state pace. Players must work intermittently, because obviously football is an intermittent sport. So it's sprint, jog, walk, recover, and not constant running. You never play football like that. This also allows the players to work across all the energy systems and that is going to prepare them because all the energy systems are stressed when they are playing football."

Solutions

Although every situation is different, knowing *what does not work* is critical in this situation. If you have an unfit player with an aerobic system that is not fully prepared for heavier loads, and they take on a heavier load than they are used to, the chances of injury increase significantly. In other words, you cannot punish a player to the point that they break down and become injured.

Instead, the goal for coaches should be to assist the player in developing a solid base so they can then progress to more high intensity training, which matches the demands of the game. Patience is important and there must also be a dialogue with the player so that they know what is required and are willing to commit to the program. Coaches must also learn to manage the situation, rather than react to it. The frustrations of the summer must be put to the side if the team is to move forward.

Planning – instead of reacting – shapes a coach's behavior towards forward planning, emotional control, and a focus on solutions. The most successful coaches, today, excel in the preparation side of preseason, and are open to new ways to schedule strength training and methods of recovery, and to work alongside their sports science staff to meet goals and objectives. In addition, if sports science staff are aware of the game model, they can both strategize on how to build fitness alongside the tactical component of the game, and it becomes much easier to implement, manage, and make decisions throughout the year.

It is not about simply loading up the player with additional training and more work, but instead developing a program that can assist them in getting back to full fitness. If unfit players are given an individual plan, which follows the principles of periodization, and can both test and challenge them appropriately, they will eventually reach a balance point where they can take on more high intensity training.

Although individual training is great for players who need to do some physical work, it is not exclusive to those players. In fact, if specialized training is only prescribed to players who are not at required fitness levels, it sends a message to the team that it is a consequence and not a positive element of your training program. There will be other players, too, who will benefit from specialized, individual training:

Confidence Strugglers – If a player is going through a difficult period, practice time becomes more important than game time. Individual training is a perfect opportunity for a player and coach to discuss new roles and responsibilities for the season ahead and allows the coach to give advice on key areas that a player can target to improve on. Once competitive games begin, not every player will be involved so certain players will need additional technical or physical work so that they can improve or maintain sharpness and be ready for when their opportunity arrives during the season.

Injured Players– Not every fitness issue during preseason is due to poor preparation. Chances are that you will have players who are coming in whilst recovering from an injury. Earlier in this book we highlighted the work of Tim Gabbett and he has also done extensive work in this area to identify if the athlete has trained enough to return to play safely. His studies have shown that when an athlete's training and playing load for a given week "spikes" above what they have been doing on average over the past four weeks, they are more likely to be injured. "Load is not the problem. It's what you've been prepared for that's the problem." Again, every player must be managed individually and some may need additional work to strengthen key areas.

Improve Culture – If individual training is only done when players are unfit or after the team loses, it becomes more reactive than proactive and is not a key part of the team culture. This would be the wrong message to send as a coach. You want players doing more and you want them associating it with driving their game to the next level. At the academy of both Liverpool and Tottenham Hostpur, they have a '10 minute rule' with their youth teams where players must work on specific aspects of their game for ten minutes before or after every session. Sometimes this will be with a coach, and sometimes not, but it is consistent with their culture which is to enhance yourself as a player every single day.

Positional Work – Many teams at youth level battle with winning versus development. For a team to be successful today, however, coaches need to be equipped to do both. Players must develop the ability to perform key skills at key moments of the game, and coaches must find new ways to teach it. In 'The Modern Soccer Coach – Position Specific Training' we looked at ways to identify, develop, and enhance the skills and functions of the modern player whatever their position and role on the pitch. Traditional training structures that center around team exercises is no longer enough for players to execute specialized technical skills under pressure.

Principles of Individual Training

The difference between additional work and specialized, individual training lies in the quality of planning, focused outcome, and buy-in from players. Coaches must have a program in place that complements their team training sessions so that players can embrace this type of training and enjoy it. Below are the key principles that should be included in the program:

Communication – The first and most important step towards effective specialized training is having great communication with players. If a coach doesn't explain the reasons for training, it will be viewed as punishment and perceived negatively. It is the responsibility of the coach to articulate the goals as precisely as possible and then work with the player to build problems into clear and mutually agreed upon training objectives.

Individualized approach – If two players at different fitness levels do a training session, there will be different responses, in the exact same way there would be at different skill levels. Any previous injury history should also be a factor in the planning process. Age must also be taken into consideration and coaches who work with young players must treat them as young players, not experienced professionals. Players may also be at different stages technically and this can lead to training being adapted accordingly.

Game Specific Exercises – It is also the responsibility of the coach to identify the specific movements for the player that translate to their position and play a key part in their game. There needs to be an understanding of the player's roles and responsibilities within the playing model, which should then provide the direction for the type of training to take place. For example, having a defender spending extra time shooting and finishing in front of goal is not the best way to manage their time.

Provide Feedback – Any player who suddenly puts more into their game than they are used to, is invariably going to want quick results. Although the game does not do 'quick fixes', a coach can substitute them for feedback on training and performance. Don't wait until mid-season or after the season for evaluations. Instead, provide regular feedback in both directions – aspects of training that are going well and things to improve.

Exercise One

This is a multi-functional individual exercise that incorporates a number of fundamental skills that a player can work on. Passing, dribbling, and shooting are all covered and this is a perfect exercise for a player looking for some extra technical work, or returning from injury and wanting different types of actions with the ball. There are a number of variables here that the coach can manage and control, depending on the player and what the objectives are. The exercise could be performed at high or low intensity, skills can be manipulated to be more difficult, distances can be altered so that more or less power is required, and time can be changed to increase or decrease the volume of work.

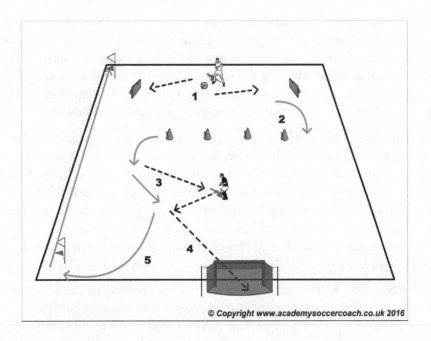

On the first station, the player is passing back and forth between two rebound boards. (The boards could be substituted for other players if you don't have the equipment). Technically, you want the ball moving quickly here so that the player in the middle always plays with two touches, one to open up in possession and one to switch the play. The player's body shape should always be sideways on. After 15-20 seconds, the coach signals and the player must then slalom through the cones. As soon as the player comes out, he/she plays a give-and-go with the coach and then shoots on goal. After the shot, the player runs around the flag and back up to the starting point.

Exercise Two

If a coach wants to add intensity to an exercise, nothing does it quite like competition. 1v1 exercises are a great way to get players pushing to their maximum and the majority of players view it as a fun activity. From a physical and conditioning viewpoint, this exercise also incorporates different types of movements within the exercise, rather than a traditional 1v1 exercise where players face each other and run straight out towards one another. As a result of this, the coach can adapt the movements and the load to suit the needs of one or both players.

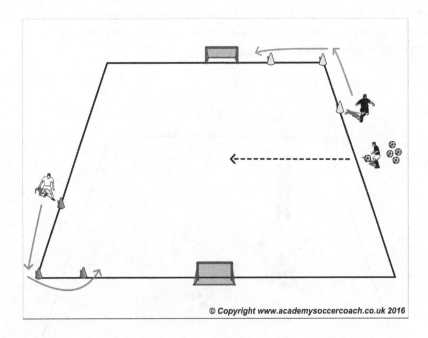

The exercise takes place in a 20x20 yard square with two players starting on the first cone. The coach is in the middle with a supply of balls. On the coach's signal, players must sprint out around the cones and then onto the field where the coach has passed a ball for both players to compete. The game then becomes a basic 1v1 game towards the opponent's goal (located at the respective end that they both started from). After a goal is scored or ball leaves the playing area, both players have 30 seconds to recover back to their starting positions before the next ball is played. They continue this for 5 balls which concludes the set. The coach can then manage the load of the players to set additional sets or make the exercise even more physically demanding.

Exercise Three

When a player is tired or unfit, technique and decision making are two areas that are impacted most. Quite often, decision making is left unexposed in training because, if the player is experienced, they can take up positions that do not necessarily expose them physically. We talked about this earlier in the book and used traditional 5v5 games where players can 'sit' in certain positions that do not require them to play outside their physical comfort zone. A breakdown in technique on the other hand, is difficult to hide when fitness levels begin to drop dramatically. In a high intensity game or exercise, a player cannot escape technical demands and if a player is continually making the same types of mistakes, it will be hard for them to break into a starting line-up or even contribute when coming off the bench.

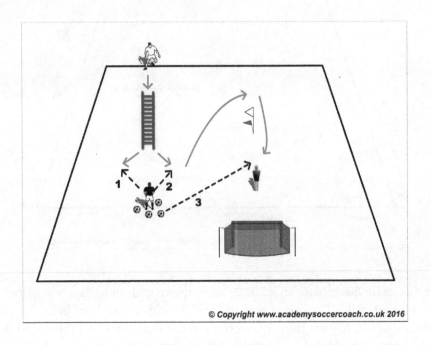

This is a technical circuit directed towards improving technique and fitness alongside one another. It allows the coach the flexibility to control both the intensity and the range of movement under which the athlete must perform. The player starts at the top of the speed ladder and accelerates through towards the coach. When they reach the end, the coach serves a ball from their hands to the player to volley back, once on their right foot and once on their left. After the two volleys, the player runs backwards towards the flag before accelerating forwards once they reach it. The coach will then pass a ball in front of the mannequin for the player to take one touch and shoot on then shoot goal. The player then has 45 seconds to recover back to the starting place before going again. After 5 balls, they have completed one set and the coach can manage the load depending on what the player needs.

The coach must manage quality control here and demand that the technical work is performed at a high level. The coach must never allow the player to slow down and plant their feet while waiting on service from the coach. Instead, the emphasis should be on checking towards the ball and performing the technical skill with forward momentum. This attention to detail will challenge the player to not only complete the exercise, but to do so at a high technical level.

Exercise Four

All heading exercises should have a physical component attached to them. It is, after all, an explosive action that requires good footwork and upper body strength. A lot of heading exercises at youth level, however, are performed with both feet on the ground. The ball is served around head height and the player does not have to jump or 'spring' into the air to deal with it effectively. As a result, players are underprepared to deal with the situations that arise in a game. If we learn to improve footwork and the understanding of how to use upper bodies as leverage, our defenders should become better in this area.

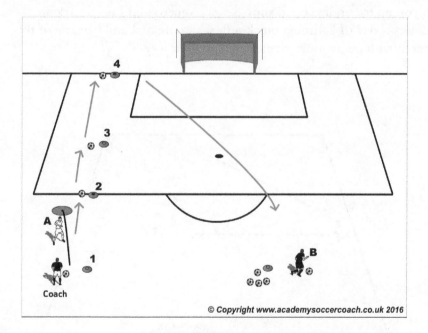

This multi-functional defensive exercise challenges the defender to perform continuous explosive actions and then transition into a 1v1 situation. Four balls are placed on four cones every six yards from the goal line. The defender starts at the first cone, facing the cone. On the signal, the defender backtracks and the coach throws the ball high for him/her to head. The goal of the defender is to head each ball over the head of the coach so they are getting both height and distance onto the headed clearance. The coach moves forward at the same speed with which the defender moves backwards and serves a ball at cones 2, 3, and 4. After the fourth header, the defender sprints from the goal line towards player B where they compete in a 1v1 situation. Player B must try to beat the defender and shoot into an empty goal. After the goal or defensive block, the defender goes back to the first cone and recovers for 45 seconds before going again.

Exercise Five

Typically, the more variables added to a finishing exercise, the more challenging it becomes for players. Both space and time have become a premium, and penalty boxes are so compact these days, that opportunities are hard to come by. The best way to combat this problem is with technical ability and quick decision making. With technical ability, it is not simply about first touch to control the ball, but rather your first touch to set you up for your second shot. Sergio Aguero and Luis Suarez are masters today of lightning quick reflexes in the box and because of this, benefit with many more chances falling their way.

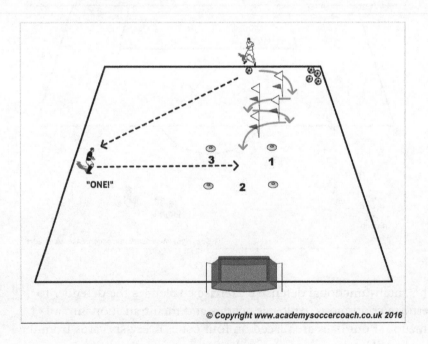

This exercise challenges the forward to make quick decisions and set themselves quickly for a shot in a variety of ways. It also works on speed and agility so that the technique is not taught in isolation. Again, the coach can modify the exercise to increase or decrease the intensity and physical demands.

The exercise takes place 25 yards from goal and includes four flags and a 5x5 yard box. The three sides of the bottom of the box are numbered one, two, and three. The forward begins the exercise by passing the ball to the coach. After the pass, the forward must slalom through the flags as quickly as possible. When the forward arrives out of the flags and into the box, the coach plays a ball into the square. When the ball is travelling to the forward, the coach calls out a number and the forward must adjust their feet and first touch accordingly. Although the forward receives the ball inside the square, their first touch must take them out at the direction of the number call. For example, in the diagram, the coach calls out number one, so the forward must come out of the left side of the square with one touch and then – once outside the square – shoot on goal. The forward has 45 seconds to recover back to the starting position before going again and repeating this for five balls.

Exercise Six

As the physical demands for a goalkeeper are greater than they have ever been, training exercises must be specific and realistic to their game. A goalkeeper traditionally was the one who was at the back of preseason runs and testing, waiting for the balls to appear before they had the opportunity to prove their worth in the team. Today, explosiveness and footskills are key requirements for a goalkeeper, not to mention decision making and range of distribution. It is up to coaches therefore to get the session content right when it comes to working with goalkeepers. Asking them to do continuous laps of the field will not necessarily make them worse, but there are more effective ways to make them better.

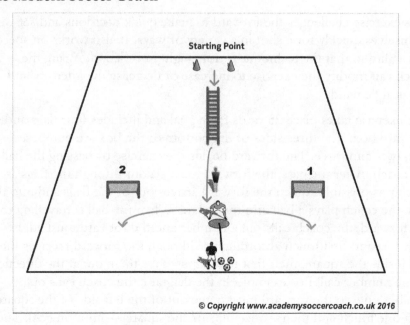

© Copyright www.academysoccercoach.co.uk 2016

Although this exercise is both physically and technically challenging, it is enjoyable for a goalkeeper because it tests them in areas where they know they will be called upon during the game. The exercise was developed by Clifton Bush and uses a speed ladder along with two mini-goals, numbered one and two. The goalkeeper begins at the starting point and, on the coach's signal, goes through the speed ladder with the correct footwork. The goalkeeper arrives into set position in front of the mannequin where they receive a volley from the coach, delivered at head height. As soon as the goalkeeper catches the volley, they must discard the ball; the coach then calls out a number for the goalkeeper to move towards. As they move towards the mini-goal of the number called, the coach delivers a second ball for the goalkeeper to save. The goalkeeper then recovers back to the starting position and performs 10 of these actions in total.

Conclusion

Every coach around the world is faced with a problem when players report for preseason unfit or not at their best. How they deal with it can have either huge benefits or ramifications to the culture of the team, and health of the players. It is not about proving a point or trying to find a scapegoat, but instead it's about accepting a challenge in your preparation, planning, session content, and the ability to learn more about a crucial area of the game that will directly impact your team.

Part of being a modern coach is embracing both new ideas and ways of working. Michael Watts believes traditional thinking is holding back too many coaches in this area. "The words 'It's pre-season… it should be hard' or 'It's pre-season… you should be sick' are the words of a soccer coach who doesn't know what they are doing." In addition, if coaches are brave enough to introduce specialized individual training as part of a team culture, players will be naturally more inclined to want to improve and not see it as punishment. It's not easy, it's not quick, and it can only take place if coaches are willing to move away from the traditional training structure. A big prize is worth a big effort. Former Manchester United assistant coach, Rene Meulensteen, believes that if players see benefit, they will commit to it. "The really top performers in any walk of life and in any sport will embrace it if you can add something to their performance that will make it better." The coaches who can adopt that type of mentality to problems, as opposed to blame or fault-finding, will find rewards where other coaches simply find more problems.

9

Shooting and Finishing

Goal scoring has always been, and always will be, the name of the game in football. If you look at any successful team in any league or tournament, chances are they will have at least one player on the 'top scorers' chart.

The ability to score goals or create something special in the opposition's penalty area will ultimately define the fate of your team, no matter how good you are defensively or in possession. As such, what role does a coach play here, and just how much impact can we have when it comes to helping your team put the ball in the back of the net?

The answer depends on whom you ask. Traditional thinking believes that we are at the mercy of players who were specifically born to score goals. Filippo Inzaghi, Raul, Robbie Fowler, and Ruud van Nistelrooy, are all examples of players throughout the history of the game who always seemed to be in the right place at the right time. They have a natural instinct in front of goal and their teams benefitted by them simply showing up. People argued that it does not matter how good a team is 'going forward', they will not win trophies until they have a 'natural goalscorer'.

A new school of thought centered around hard work and improvement, however, has gained considerable momentum in recent years. In *The Modern Soccer Coach – Position Specific Training* I argued that the 'natural goalscorer' is nothing more than a myth. Players have the ability to redirect the path of both themselves and their teams, and there are no better examples in the modern game than Jamie Vardy and Harry Kane. Here are two players who have made such an impact on the Premier League goalscoring charts over the past two seasons, that the world's media cannot seem to work out where they have come from. Although at 22 years of age, Kane has found his goals at the highest level well before Vardy (who is currently 29) both players have spent a number of years with different clubs at lower levels, without making anywhere near the same impact. So what exactly was it that gave them the breakthrough, and catapulted their careers to the world stage? Was it luck, poor opposition, right place at the right time, or have they actually taken responsibility and ownership to change they way that they work and, in doing so, have elevated their games to another level?

According to the players themselves it may have more to do with a different approach and new levels of commitment to their work, rather than their skill and talent. Vardy himself admitted, "The secret is just lots and lots of hard work and practice, and the motivation that this is exactly what I want to be doing. It's putting it all into the practice on the training field, then making sure it's there on match day." Harry Kane credited a similar approach when asked about his goalscoring feats. "Hard work, patience, belief and when the chance came, making sure I took it."

For some reason, we seem reluctant to believe that hard work and smart work on the training ground could actually deliver more goals, but that is exactly what happened, and their belief that it could be done is exactly what fuelled their motivation. Of course, talent does exist. You cannot become an elite player without it, but maybe its definition is not as clear as we believe it to be. With the help of acclaimed authors including Carol Dweck and Matthew Syed, we are now redefining talent as something you are not born with, but rather something you develop with the help of hard work, purposeful practice, and a "growth mindset". Kane and Vardy have a great amount of ability and physical qualities, but it's easy to sit back and point at talent as the difference maker, when it is in fact how people actually use it that makes the difference.

Now let's look at the impact that coaches have had when both players 'found their form' and see if it was down to luck or design.

Leicester City coach, Claudio Ranieri, is no stranger to working with world-class talent and goalscorers in particular. Throughout his career, he has worked with some of the greatest attacking players from the 1990s to the modern era: Careca, Daniel Fonseca, Diego Milito, Francesco Totti, Allesandro Del Pierio, Jimmy Floyd Hasselbaink, Caludio Lopez, and Gabriel Batistuta. What is even more remarkable than the quality of that list is the fact that each player finished in the top three of the goalscorers' chart in their respective leagues while working under Ranieri. Is the Italian coach lucky enough to stumble upon the world's best forwards when he takes a job or does he somehow find a way to extract every ounce from their ability? The evidence points to the latter.

Mauricio Pochettino – Harry Kane's coach at Spurs – on the other hand, has not necessarily specialized in working with world-class talent, as much as he has implemented a style of play that perhaps brings something extra out of the ordinary. He is a much more offensive force than Kane's previous coaches, Andre Villas-Boas and Tim Sherwood, neither of whom saw enough in the young Englishman to trust him with regular playing time. Pace and dynamism have always been cornerstones of Pochettino's attacking systems, with forwards like Kane benefitting from free flowing attacking play. There is no doubt that Kane has thrived under Pochettino's system and the young English forward has also learnt one or two things about the application required to become a top player from his intense, demanding coach.

Both Pochettino and Ranieri have shown that, as a coach, it is certainly possible to have a huge impact on both a player and team's ability to score goals. Maybe you help a player achieve greatness through extra work, a system of play, or maybe you attract those players to your team through recruitment and your reputation as an ambitious coach. We tend to attract what we are, and forward-thinking coaches who take risks usually seem to find attacking players who share those characteristics on the field. This can also be directly related to preseason. If we are sitting around, hoping for our team to come back in good physical condition, are we also applying the same principles to goalscoring? If we are, we need to acknowledge it and look to change. One of the best uses of a coach's time during the pre-season period is to increase a team's competence in key result areas and two of these areas are the creation of chances, and scoring goals.

Making It Realistic

The consistent message in this book has been that it is not good enough to simply add a certain exercise or session to your program. As coaches, it is so important that we pay close attention to when and how we do it. That is how it will have the maximum effect and have a better chance of being transferred to games.

A shooting session introduced after a tough session may be disadvantageous for the team as players will be more susceptible to injury because of fatigue. Likewise, if shooting is just something a team does at the end of every session, players may lose focus and view it as just a fun activity. Neither way works for a coach or the team. Here are the best ways to make your shooting and finishing as realistic as possible.

Competition – There is no doubt that scoring goals takes high individual levels of desire and determination. Experts on TV will often say that a forward rose above a defender to score because he "wanted it more". Although high levels of competitiveness can come from within, they can be enhanced by coaches who facilitate it through their training structure. Competitive sessions raise tempo, intensity, and help players focus on winning. Former Liverpool Academy director, Steve Heighway, believes that this approach has always been at the heart of the club's successful youth policy. "We must never lose an opportunity to fire the players' competitive edge."

Clock – A number of shooting opportunities that present themselves during games are squandered because players panic or are not ready to take advantage of the opportunity. If the coach does not opt for defensive pressure, time should be used in its place. This will improve reaction times and awareness levels. Once a player is comfortable performing attacking technical skills at full speed, they can transfer them to the game a lot more easily.

Variety and Understanding of the Skill – We are seeing a higher variety of shots in the modern game than ever before. Top players today are putting extra topspin on the ball which is causing the ball to whip, dip, curve and swerve like never before. Coaching points used to be centered around a planted foot, head over the ball, and follow through. Now, the technical demands have expanded to body shape, art of disguise, manipulating the ball, and turning quickly to create space. Coaches must put their players in more difficult situations within their practice structure so they can not only learn different techniques, but also develop the understanding and confidence of when to use them.

Angles – Too many shooting exercises take place under perfect conditions. They take place in the middle of the goal and allow the player to take a long run up so they can focus and hit the target. Of course, the game itself looks very different. The edge of the box is the most congested area so chances there will be few and far between. Instead, attacking players must learn how to be dangerous from difficult angles so they can become more of threat to defenders and goalkeepers.

Fatigue Related – Similar to the possession element of the game, one of the best ways to test and challenge technical ability is to add fatigue. A forward might have to wait 89 minutes to get their only chance on goal, so it is important that technique does not crumble when fatigue enters the equation. In addition, the physical demands for a center forward are also high with the majority of teams requiring every outfield player to commit to the defensive system, which may include pressing or channeling play to one side – both of which require high energy levels.

Exercise One

Sometimes coaches can manipulate the conditions of certain exercises so that they get more physical output from the players, sometimes without them realizing it. Exercise one is one of my favourite preseason exercises and combines long-distance running, shooting, and also has a real competitive element that allows players the opportunity to bond and work together. It may look like a fun shooting exercise but in reality, players will be tested to their maximum both aerobically and anaerobically.

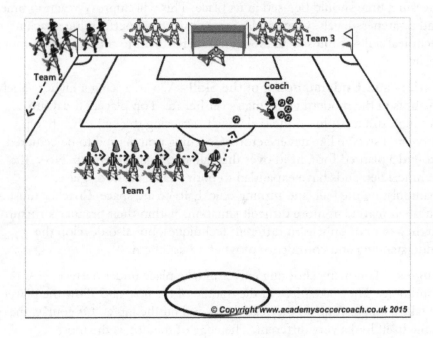

The squad is split into three teams. One team starts in the corner (black), the second behind the goal (white), and the third team (stripes) on a cone each just outside the penalty area. You will need a goalkeeper, half a field, and a good supply of balls to keep the exercise moving along. All groups work at the same time.

The team in stripes are up first to shoot. Each player starts in a push-up position on a separate yellow cone. On the coach's signal, the players must all perform a push-up at each cone, sliding over quickly from one to the next. When the players reach the last cone, they must get up quickly and the coach will pass them a ball. After the player shoots, they must start again on the first cone and perform 5 push-ups (one at each cone) before they get another chance to shoot.

At the same time, the black team must sprint around the full pitch and return to their starting spot. The speed of the black team will determine how long the striped team shoot for. When the last player returns to the starting spot, time expires for the striped team. Therefore, the quicker the black team runs, the less time the other team has to shoot. The white team are resting but must make sure that the coach always has a supply of balls. One of the white players must also keep the score. After the striped team shoots, they recover behind the goal, the black team now shoots, and the white team must run around the pitch.

Progressions:

There are a number of variations to the exercise. You can change the type of running from endurance to sprint work. You can also vary the action performed on each cone. From a technical standpoint, you can change service or challenge the players to score in a different way.

Exercise Two

Contrary to the shouts from the sidelines on a Saturday, not every shot from outside the box is a 'good effort' or 'good idea'. The higher the level, the more scarce that opportunities become in the final third and an extra pass or two can sometimes be a much better option than a rushed, off-balance shot. In the majority of traditional shooting exercises, the player never has to work for the shot. Sometimes they have to perform an action and the ball is there waiting for them, and at other times they have a set shot in a set position. One of the most difficult skills for attacking players, however, is positioning themselves effectively or creating the right kind of shot that they want. Lionel Messi and Arjen Robben are great examples of players who are able to create the right position off the dribble where they manufacture their favorite type of shot. Frank Lampard was another player who turned timing and arriving at the right position, at the right time, into an art form. This is a great game for combination play around the box, speed of thought with technical ability, and developing an understanding of what is a good shot and what isn't.

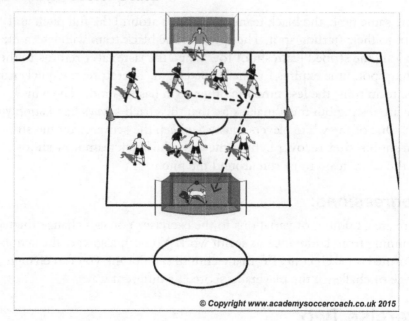

© Copyright www.academysoccercoach.co.uk 2015

The exercise involves eight players, with two goalkeepers, and takes place inside a 36 yard, or two 18-yard boxes. Teams are organized into a 3v1 on each side, in favor of the defensive team. All players are restricted to their own area. Play starts from a goalkeeper and the objective is for the 3 players to create a shot on their half of the field. The role of the lone forward, defensively, is to press and try to keep them out of a certain area where they want to shoot (e.g. the middle of the field). Defending players on the other team can block the shot but cannot leave their own half. The lone forward on the other side is looking for rebounds from the shot but can also be used as a player to combine with, or pass to.

Progressions:

- To increase the tempo of the game, implement a four pass maximum on the team in possession.
- Award two points for a goal from a rebound, as this will allow the defensive team to create good habits if they allow the shot on goal.
- If a goal is scored from a first time shot it is worth three points. You don't want players waiting for the perfect circumstance to shoot. If they are in the right position, at the right time, they should always have a go!

Exercise Three

Without a limit on time or a competitive element, shooting exercises are in danger of becoming unrealistic or irrelevant in the context of the real game. We have already addressed how competition and time add intensity, but they also challenge players to focus on the small technical details that are vital in shooting. This is a shooting competition which includes a number of variables that are important in shooting. The service, the first touch, and the acceleration required before and after the shot, all challenge players to perform. Players are constantly moving throughout the exercise and are tested on both their left and right sides. In addition, the element of pressure added by team competition means that composure in front of goal becomes a key factor too.

The exercise is set up on one side of the field, with players organized into two teams; the white team at one end and the black team at the other. Players on both ends position themselves with a ball each at cones A and C. One player from each team starts at cones B and D, at two gates that are placed 18 yards from goal, without a ball. On the coach's signal, both teams start at the same time with a pass from player A to player B, through the gate. Player B has one touch to set the ball forward, and must finish on goal with the second touch. If the first touch is too heavy, the goalkeeper can come off their line and collect it or make a save. Player B's first touch does not have to go through the gate, but if the initial pass from A to B does not, the goal does not count. After the shot on goal, player C passes to player D and the same action takes place on the other side. At the same time, player A replaces player B and player B goes to the back of the other line. After four minutes, the goals are totalled by both teams and a winner is determined.

Progressions:

- The initial pass must be played in the air and the player at the top of the box now has a different technical challenge.
- Instead of going to the back of the other line after the shot, the player makes their way to the penalty spot and acts as a rebounder for the other side. This will encourage players to shoot across goal as the possibility of getting a rebound in front of goal dramatically increases.

Exercise Four

Another key area overlooked in many shooting exercises is the decision making associated with finishing in the final third. Being told when to shoot and how to shoot is effective coaching at a youth level, but as players progress in the game, the ability to make the correct decision under pressure will play a major part in the speed of an individual's ascent. This is a fun, competitive game designed by NSCAA Director of Coaching Education, Ian Barker, that challenges players to make decisions in an overload situation and finish on goal. The transitional nature of the game requires players to perform with speed and intensity that will also test them technically.

The exercise takes place in a 25x40 area with three teams of four players and two goalkeepers. The field is split in half with six balls distributed across the field, on both sides. The first attacking team (white team) have two players on each side of the field. The other two teams are defending and both take up positions in either half of the field. Each attacking pair has six balls they must take to goal. One player from the defensive team in each half can come in and defend so that it becomes a 2v1 towards goal. The same defensive player cannot defend two balls in a row. After the six balls, rotate the teams on each side and keep score throughout so that a winning team is determined at the end.

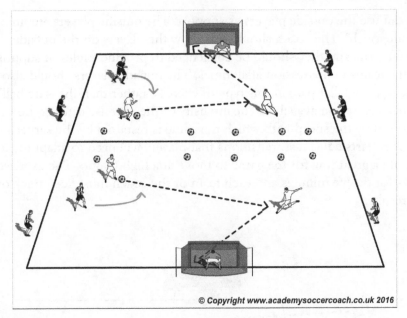

© Copyright www.academysoccercoach.co.uk 2016

Progressions:

- Add a time limit of 90 seconds for teams to complete their six balls or 15 seconds for each attack.
- If a goalkeeper or defender wins the ball and successfully plays it to one of the players on the outside, the attacking team loses a goal.
- Allow two defensive players in, to create a 2v2 situation with every ball.

Exercise Five

This is a great exercise to rejuvenate your team after a couple of tough days training. The physical demands are not too steep, in terms of running distances or number of sprints required, but the competitive aspect will drive the tempo and intensity required for pre-season training. This game is fun but certainly a lot more difficult than it initially looks. Pressure plays a big part in this exercise, from both the opposition and the environment.

The game exercise takes place inside the penalty area with twelve players organized into four teams of three. There is also a goalkeeper and a server on top of the 18-yard box with a supply of balls. Two teams start inside the penalty area in a 3v3 game. The rules are simple: the first team to score wins the game. The winning team stays on the field and the losing team rotates with another on the outside. The team in possession of the ball can use the outside players as support. The outside players are limited to 'one touch'. The coach should not allow the players on the outside to remain static and they should be challenged to provide angles of support for the teams in possession at all times. The outside players should also be looking for a killer pass in this type of exercise rather than the 'safe ball' to the nearest option available. The intensity of the exercise can also be increased by the speed with which the game is restarted by the server. Quick restarts equal fast transitions that players will need to adapt to, and they are a great way for the game to move at a high tempo. The exercise flows for twelve minutes and each team or the coach must keep track of the results.

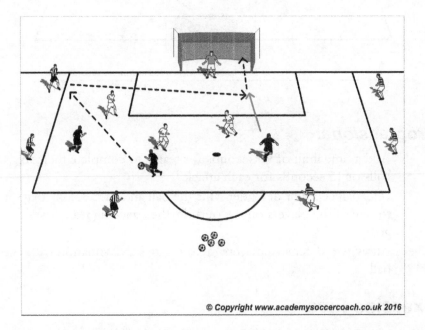

© Copyright www.academysoccercoach.co.uk 2016

Progressions:

- After a goal is scored, challenge players to react and transition quickly by starting the next game in five seconds. This will keep the games moving quickly and requires teams to communicate with each other so they can get organized quickly.

Exercise Six

If the goal of a particular session is to work more on fitness, the coach may want to increase the physical demands of any shooting exercise. To do this, you can manipulate the conditions of an exercise with transition and competition. This is a technical shooting exercise that progresses into a fast-flowing, competitive, attack versus defense battle. It takes place in a 20x30 yards area, with two teams and two goalkeepers. Both teams start in opposite corners with a ball each. There are two coaches or servers in the middle who will remain there throughout the first part of the exercise.

The exercise starts when the first player on each side dribbles, simultaneously, towards the mannequin. On the approach to the mannequin, they play a pass into the server, accelerate forward into space, get the return and then shoot on goal. The next player cannot go until the previous player has sprinted through the gate. The exercise lasts for four minutes and the number of goals scored are recorded so there will be a winner.

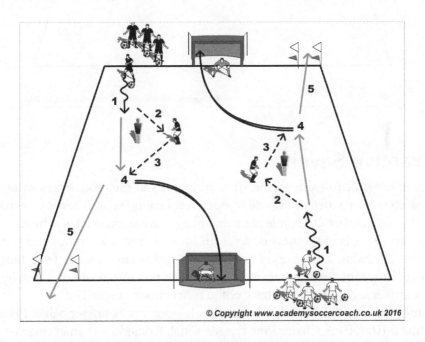

© Copyright www.academysoccercoach.co.uk 2016

The progression of this game now occurs when we combine the technical exercise with direct competition. Again, two teams are organized on either side of the field with a ball each. This time, however, the gates along with the servers and the mannequins are moved towards the middle and placed parallel to each other. The exercise begins when the first player in white dribbles past the mannequins and shoots on goal. Directly after the shot, the same player must transition into being a defender and player 2 from the black team attacks the other goal. After player 2 shoots, he/she must defend, and so on. Every player returns to their own team after defending once. The first team to score ten goals wins.

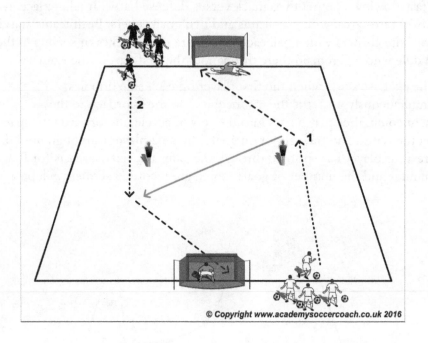

Exercise Seven

It is impossible to study the art of scoring goals in the modern era without looking at how Cristiano Ronaldo operates. Having scored his 500th career goal in September 2015, it is clear that his game has evolved and he can now score goals in a variety of ways. In his early years, as an out-and-out winger, Ronaldo leaned upon his 1v1 skills and ability to score from long range. In recent years, however, he has developed into more of a penalty box striker where his goals have come from closer range. The combination of both approaches makes his practically unstoppable. Prior to the 2016 UEFA Champions League Final, Ronaldo has an average of 8.2 shots per game, with 1.6 goals scored. Outside the box, there is no hesitation or doubt in his mind to hit the target. Inside the box, he has been rewarded for his movement and his desire to get into the right areas at the right time. This multi-functional shooting and finishing exercise is developed with Ronaldo in mind. It combines long range shooting ability with the speed and commitment required to get into goalscoring positions within the box.

The exercise takes place with three goals. Players are split into two teams and start at A and B. Two wide players (striped jerseys) are located at C and D and two servers take a position alongside the speed ladders. Goalkeepers are optional. The first players at A and B begin the exercise by passing to their servers, and going through the speed ladder. When they are coming to the end of their footwork through the ladders, the servers return the pass in front of them for players A and B to accelerate through and finish with a shot on goal. The first ball to hit the back of the net scores a point for their team.

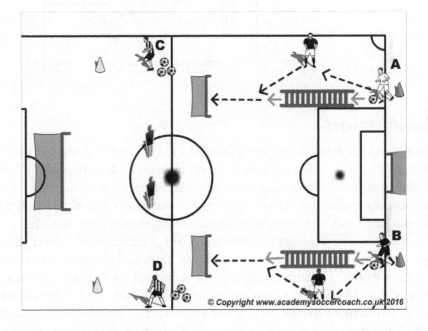

After the shooting segment, the exercise continues as both players must sprint around the furthest mannequin located in the center circle. As soon as the first player reaches the mannequin, one of the wide players (player C below) starts dribbling the ball at full speed towards the cone and, as soon as they pass the cone, they cross the ball into the box. The first player from team A or B who gets in the box has to finish into an open goal. If both players enter the box at the same time, they must compete for the ball and finish on goal. This goal is worth two points. The exercise restarts at the beginning, and wide players switch roles. Keep track of all points scored and there must be a winner after five minutes.

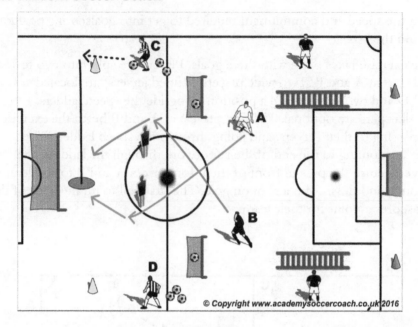

Conclusion

The playing model that the coach develops for his or her team, must have a detailed, effective plan on how to create chances and score goals. Maybe it's the strength of the tactical system, or maybe it's good mentoring or 'man-management' that leads to players embracing positional work on the training pitch and accepting more responsibility during a game. Either way, the coach must be prepared to work with, challenge, and develop their attacking players. Not every coach does it, mostly because it is easier to wish they had a 'natural goalscorer' or even criticize the one who they thought was. In addition to natural ability, it takes hard work, smart work and a commitment to scoring goals at a high level. Thomas Edison said it best, "Opportunity is missed by most people because it is dressed in overalls and looks like work."

Another reason for the importance of shooting and finishing during pre-season is the spark it provides to teams. Coaches cannot cheat time and pre-season training can be a long few weeks, both mentally and physically. If the work is always centered around running, defensive shapes, and possession principles, players become drained. Similar to games-based training, shooting sessions can act as a spark that can re-ignite energy levels. Without passion and energy, teams will never make it through a full season, so it is up to the coach to protect that energy with high-tempo exercises and enjoyable sessions.

10

Back to the Culture

No matter how fit your players are, even with the best coaching and training exercises, the success of the team lies squarely on the shoulders of the environment we create and maintain. In this book, we have identified the importance of a tactical playing model, looked at numerous exercises to work through, studied how to develop match fitness, established the responsibilities of the coaching staff, and examined the role which sports science plays towards keeping players healthy. Although these are all critical components of pre-season training, the key for coaches is how to connect them together and create buy-in from our team. Our final step in this book is to look at how to do this in order to maximize your impact as a coach. Without the players totally embracing every aspect of the program, and driving it themselves, the team will never realize its true potential. Even one of the most tactically astute coaches around, Jose Mourinho, acknowledges the importance of player buy-in ahead of coaching instruction. "It's more difficult to change mentality than to change tactics."

In Chapter Two, we looked at the importance of culture and how to create it. It is undoubtedly one of the hottest topics in coaching at the minute. Although it seems that teams who win are commended for the strength of their culture (while the teams that lose are pinpointed as lacking it completely) it is much more complex than that. Winning cultures come in all kinds of shapes and sizes. Our goal is to identify practical ways to develop it in the context of pre-season training, and use it as a competitive advantage for our team.

Team culture is defined as the expression of a team's values and beliefs about performance and competition. Whether they are aware of it, or not, every team has one and it is either created with purpose and intent, or left to be shaped by the players. Either way, the coach is responsible for it. No matter how many winning slogans are written on locker room walls, if negativity, excuses, and poor punctuality are not addressed by the coach, they will hijack team culture and shape it in a different way.

Winning Culture Characteristics

Many coaches fall into a trap of associating culture directly with one performance or result. The reality is that the stronger the culture, the more time it has to develop and the more work that goes into it. There is also no 'one size fits all' version of it, and it must be designed to complement a coach's values, player characteristics, and other factors. We will now look at the 'cultural themes' from four of the most successful and unique cultures that have separated themselves from the competition, before examining how that culture would apply in the soccer world.

1. The Cause

There is arguably no culture in world sport as strong as that of the All-Blacks. New Zealand's famous rugby team have recorded a staggering 75% win rate over the past 100 years, the highest in any sport. But despite that remarkable achievement, the All-Blacks culture is focused on something a lot bigger than wins and losses.

How can a country with only 4.7 million people continually dominate against countries with dramatically higher populations and established professional leagues? The answer is more to do with their standards and less to do with their talent. Even when they won the 2015 World Cup, their team culture created more headlines than the final itself when Sonny Bill Williams handed over his winner's medal to a young child in the crowd. Their purpose-driven culture extends to their mantra "Better People Make Better All-Blacks" with two simple but powerful team goals: 1. Leave the jersey in a better place and 2. Leave everything out on the field.

World Cup-winning Captain, Richie McCaw, believes that living up to their culture is tougher than most games. "That legacy is much more intimidating that any opposition." The goals of winning every game *and* leaving the jersey in a better position than you received it, is the motivation for every player to go above and beyond on the field (and in their preparation).

In the outstanding book, *Legacy*, author James Kerr spent a year inside the All Black's team environment, looking extensively at how their team culture is formed, maintained, and strengthened. Early in his journey, Kerr experienced the team leaving a locker room spotless as players themselves took responsibility for 'sweeping the sheds'. When asked why this was important, a team member said, "Because no one looks after the All-Blacks. The All-Blacks look after themselves." This collective attitude extends to training hard, eating right, sleeping right, and sacrificing personal glory for the benefit of the team. Kerr also writes about how the players are given a book when they first become an All-Black. The first pages show jerseys from historic New Zealand teams while the rest of the pages are blank, waiting on the player himself to fill them with new memories. There is no doubt that the extraordinary environment creates extraordinary standards, which consistently leads to extraordinary results.

If we are looking for a soccer-version of the All-Black culture, the obvious one that stands out is FC Barcelona. Even though they have produced some of the greatest players, their slogan "Mes que un club" (More than a club), tells you a little about their identity and who they represent. It refers to the club's commitment to matters beyond the soccer pitch and includes both social and political affairs. The slogan itself was created in 1968, and, with the help of the great Johan Cruyff, the club established a strong identity, both on and off the field. People expect them to play with a certain style and also expected certain results, which has seen them become the biggest club in the world. Not only have they evolved, they are now the drivers of evolution within the sport.

The challenge for the club in recent times has been more a question of maintaining and driving forward a successful culture, than simply building one. This has been a problem for other clubs with successful histories and team cultures; they often struggle when coaches change. Liverpool (Dalglish), Manchester United (Ferguson), and AC Milan (Capello) are examples of clubs who have taken a step backwards when a coach who implemented a successful culture has left.

During his time at the Nou Camp, Pep Guardiola produced a brand of football that was as close to perfection as you will ever see. His replacement, Luis Enrique has therefore been faced with the difficult task of culture progression. Although he played at Barcelona, Luis Enrique, has changed their system slightly, but the principles and style are still the foundation for the club. He has kept the traditional values of the club at the center of his work, while at the same time adapting to the strengths of his players and the opposition. Enrique is proof that you can still build on top of success and manage both the culture of the club, with the demands of the job. "We tend to romanticize things in the past. No two things are the same; every team has its own time. A coach's job is to get the best out of the players."

2. Do Extra

Great Britain's professional cycling team, Team Sky, targeted 'marginal gains' as an area to build their new culture around. It involved identifying small areas where you can make improvements, which ultimately add up to make a big difference to performance. When Sir Dave Brailsford became British Cycling Performance Director, he was determined to turn every aspect of the sport into an advantage for his team. "The whole principle came from the idea that if you broke down everything you could think of, that goes into riding a bike, and then improved it by 1%, you will get a significant increase when you put it all together."

Sky actively pursued 1 per cent improvements in areas that were overlooked by their competitors and nothing was left to chance. One of the best examples was when they took the most comfortable pillows on the road to hotels with them. This attention to detail had a dramatic impact on their culture and accelerated their growth. The culture dictated that there was no such thing as weakness, but rather new ways to improve.

No British team had ever won a Tour De France, so Brailsford set a goal to win one within five years. By focusing intensely on marginal gains, they actually did it in year three and then went on to win three times in four years. In addition, the Great Britain national cycling team (which Brailsford oversaw until 2014) won 16 gold medals at the last two Olympic Games (2012, 2008). British cycling has not only changed how their cyclists work, they have changed how they think every single day. Thoughts drive choices, choices drive habits, habits drive consistent behaviors, and consistent behaviors drive the performance.

In soccer terms, this requires a coach to analyze, question, and look to improve everything they do and question it. There are a number of 'little things' that combine to make a big difference in games and training sessions. However, marginal gains are only important if we take care of the maximal gains.

When England Women's Head Coach, Mark Sampson took the positon, he set about analyzing exactly what it would take for England to win the 2015 World Cup in Canada. During a presentation to 'Inspire Coach Education', Sampson explained that although they had 18 months to prepare, they only had 25 hours on the training pitch and 50 days when the team would be together on camp. Along with his staff, he collected the specifics and statistical information of his team and compared it directly against the best teams in the world. This analysis included GPS and OPTA data of teams, and predicted how many goals it would take, and even how many games they would have to win in extra time. No detail was too small. Sampson then created a unique system with an intense focus on both small and big gains. "I'm a massive believer in marginal gains. The way sport is going and how professional it is, finding little ways to get ahead is important. But fundamentally, don't forget what's smacking you right in the face. If there's marginal gains to be had, take them, but don't forget the massive wins. Don't think that you can't make massive changes and change an area by 20 per cent."

Sampson pinpointed two areas of marginal gains (technical and tactical) but combined them with two areas of 'massive gains' (psychology and social). These areas then became focal points for Sampson, his staff, and his team throughout their preparation. At the World Cup, the team spirit of England did provide a competitive advantage and their culture helped bring them within seconds of making a World Cup Final for the first time in their history.

3. Toughness

Every coach wants players who love to compete, but NFL Seattle Seahawks Head Coach, Pete Carroll, has gone one step further and actually created a culture around embracing 'grit', and excelling in the actual process of hard work. Quite simply, his team embrace and specialize in the things that other teams don't particularly want to do.

Carroll feels that it has a contagious effect on everyone within his program. "It's all about passion, perseverance, resilience, the sense that you won't be denied. Can you help somebody feel a little more passionate? ... Can you inspire people to never let their guard down, to always be bringing their best?"

Not only has this created an identity for the team to connect with, it has also driven self-image for current and future players. If the Seattle Seahawks want you on their roster, you must be a mentally tough player. The benefits not only include positive self-image, but also mutual respect amongst teammates. Star player Richard Sherman explained, "They won't fail. They won't lose. They just won't quit. When you've got guys who won't quit and you've got 53 of them… you've got an issue for a lot of teams."

Like any skill or technique involved in American football, Carroll also believes that 'grit' can be developed and has acquired the help of psychologist Angela Duckworth to help teach it to the players. Through her intensive studies, she has found that passion and perseverance are bigger predictors of success than talent and IQ.

Creating a team identity centered around hard work and toughness is something Diego Simeone has done very successfully with Atletico Madrid. Before he became head coach in 2011, they had won only two trophies in 15 years. Under his leadership, they have claimed five trophies in as many years. The Argentinian coach has no doubts as to the driving force. "For Atleti to keep on winning we can only do one thing – that is to work and fight. It's not enough to have talent at Atletico Madrid. At other clubs it is, but we can't sign superstars and have to look for players with a good work ethic."

Simeone leads the way with his energy on the sidelines, intensity on the training field, and tough reputation from his playing days, where his style was once described as "holding a knife between his teeth." Although there are times Simeone crosses the line of ethical behavior during games, he deserves a huge amount of credit for how he has shaped the mentality of his team.

As coaches, we tend to go looking for players to lead our culture, without understanding the pivotal role which we play ourselves. In his book, *The 21 Laws of Leadership*, John C. Maxwell discusses the 'Law of Magnetism' where, as leaders, "We tend not to attract who we want. We attract who we are." In the same way, coaches who do not model commitment and 'grit' certainly won't attract it in their players. That is why players tend to follow the person *before* they follow the plan.

4. Character

Rather than focusing on behaviors, San Antonio Spurs head coach, Greg Poppovich, goes right to the source and focuses on the character and personality of each player within his team. With five NBA titles and the league record for consecutive winning seasons, Popovich's coaching philosophy is centered around traditional values. Instead of focusing on systems or technique, he looks for players who are humble, can take on information, and accept adversity. In his eyes, talent is as common as table salt in the NBA. In a league where the *average* salary is $5 million, Popovich refuses to change his principles as he works to develop strong leaders whose character matches their talent, "You can only get so much satisfaction from the ball going through the hoop. There's gotta be more."

When ESPN's Baxter Holmes asked him what he looked for in players, Popovich responded, "For us, it's easy. We're looking for character, but what the hell does that mean? We're looking for people — and I've said it many times — [who] have gotten over themselves, and you can tell that pretty quickly. You can talk to somebody for four or five minutes, and you can tell if it's about them, or if they understand that they're just a piece of the puzzle. So we look for that. A sense of humor is a huge thing with us. You've got to be able to laugh. You've got to be able to take a dig, give a dig — that sort of thing. And [you have to] feel comfortable in your own skin that you don't have all the answers. [We want] people who are participatory. We need people who can handle information and not take it personally because in most of these organizations, there's a big divide. All of a sudden, the wall goes up between management and coaching and everybody is ready to blame back and forth and that's the rule rather than the exception. It just happens. But that's about people. It's about finding people who have all of those qualities. So, we do our best to look for that and when somebody comes, they figure it out pretty quick."

Modern soccer coaching is not about throwing away traditional values that were important in a previous generation. It's about maintaining those key principles and adapting to work with a new generation of player, in a changing game. No one did this better than Sir Alex Ferguson. Whereas many successful coaches in the 1990s struggled to adapt to the modern game, Ferguson always stayed one step ahead with his approach to sports science, sports psychology, and the recruitment of innovative staff to keep the ideas on training sessions fresh. He did not, however, change his views on what made players successful in any era. In his book, *Leading*, he recalls how the best players – from Bryan Robson in the 1980s right up to Cristiano Ronaldo today – shared certain character traits. "The very best have a deeply ingrained capacity for industry, and intuitively grasp that if you can connect talent and work, you can achieve so much."

Nothing frustrates committed and disciplined players more than being placed with others who lack those same qualities, and that is where Sir Alex Ferguson set his competitive advantage. "If you can assemble a team of 11 talented players who concentrate intently during training sessions, take care of their diet and bodies, get enough sleep and show up on time, then you are halfway to winning a trophy. It is always astonishing how many clubs are incapable of doing this."

The Role of the Coach

Henry Kissinger defined leadership as the art of, "taking people where they would not have gone themselves." There are plenty of good coaches who can do this on the pitch, but the great coaches of the modern era separate themselves by their ability to influence both a player's lifestyle and their mindset, as well as their performance. To move from good to great in this regard, we must look at a coach as more of a leader, rather than a technician on the field. Below are the areas where successful modern coaches tend to excel.

Communication

The majority of coaches know what they want, both on and off the field, but quite a few struggle to relate their vision to their team and staff. By communicating effectively, a team tends to trust a coach even more and commit a lot more easily to the hard work and sacrifice required to be successful. Performance coach and author of *The Pressure Principle*, Dave Alred, views how we speak as one of the most underrated aspects of coaching. "Language is the currency by which we think things through. Most coaching courses spend a lot of time on the technical side of what they are doing but not how it is communicated to the learner."

This is often put to the test after a defeat or a poor performance and emotional control has become a prerequisite for any coach who is ambitious to remain in the game a long time. If you lose a game or two, guiding your team through the process without 'losing' the players can be challenging but is so important. Soccer is an emotional game and pressure can add another dynamic to it which can play havoc with the temperament and poise of a coach. Bournemouth coach, Eddie Howe, is deliberate about how he speaks to his team especially if things have not gone well. "I'm very aware about what I say. I have to be, because a wrong word or poorly executed sentence can do a lot of damage." Profanity is becoming unacceptable in a number of youth and college environments, and rightly so. Today, the message players hear means more than the words that are spoken, and the best coaches also understand that the goal of all communication is action.

Relationships

The ability of the coach to get everyone working together is also essential for the success of the team. Only when players feel good about the coach and trust them will they commit to the process rather than simply comply. The pace of life is so hurried today that most coaches and players are rushing off to something else immediately after a session or team event.

Getting to know our players has become something of a lost art but coaches still need to make time to sit down and talk with players about their game and their lives. That is why one of the greatest things a coach can give a player is their time, as players want to feel special and appreciated.

Building relationships at all levels takes work, discipline and a dedication to the process. Although it can be a difficult job for a coach to balance being demanding and empathetic – it can be done. In his first season at Liverpool, Adam Lallana praised Jurgen Klopp for his ability to do both.

"People speak about the hugs he seems to give everyone but sometimes that means a lot to a player. It can make you feel wanted and shows he appreciates the hard work you have just put into a game. He demands hard work. He demands 100%, He doesn't do passive."

At youth level, the coach also has a responsibility to mentor players and teach them how to deal with problems in a calm and rational state. Rather than reacting to situations, coaches today must think through multiple scenarios and consider the impact of their decisions on the team.

Commitment

One of the biggest complaints from coaches about players today is that they are not committed enough. This is what separates the doers from the dreamers. Showing your commitment sets the example for all your players to follow and leads to greater respect from the team. Chelsea academy coach, Joe Edwards, believes that it is a core requirement of their staff. "If we are continually asking the players to be the best that they can be, to give 100% every day and continue to learn and develop – then we have to lead by example as coaches."

Commitment has many levels and is not just about logging hours or telling everyone how hard you are working. Although it can be defined to all players and staff during pre-season, commitment is measured at the midway point when obstacles, fatigue, and the roller-coaster nature of a season takes its toll. It is then that the players draw energy and inspiration from the coach who still brings the same level of passion and excellence that they had on day one. The path to our goal will never be straight and every team faces adversity at some stage of the season. When the pressure is on, or when bad times arrive, it can be a testing time. The coach must be prepared to adapt and move on with a positive mindset.

Preparation Checklist

There is more to pre-season preparation than preparing training sessions and tactical plans. The coach plays a pivotal role and must look at how they plan on maximizing their potential as a leader throughout the season. Below is a checklist that highlights key areas

1. Diet – Just as a balanced diet is important for the players, it also plays a key role in the success of a coach. A small drop in hydration levels leads to a 20 per cent drop in mental function. Similarly, healthy food can both improve energy levels and sharpen your mind.

2. Sleep – Recent studies have shown that sleep deprivation carries risks not only to health, but also to decision making. It can also damage empathy levels, how to process information, and the ability to deal with people. Coaches who fail to get adequate sleep risk cognitive failure.

3. Fitness – Coaches should be able to live up to the standards that they require from their players. This includes being physically fit. Sports Performance Specialist, Allister McCaw said, "The best example is yourself. Great coaches have a great energy and how can you expect to have a great energy if you are not taking care of yourself?"

4. Communication Systems – Formal and informal methods should be established including the ways information will be transferred from the coach to both staff and players. With great communication, everyone will know what they are working for and their exact role in helping the team achieve it.

5. Define Success – Everyone wants the quick fix and the majority of teams set a goal of winning the league or cup at the end of the season. There should, however, be a focus on the process and coaches must be clear about the outcome you want your team to achieve, the impact you will make, and the difference you will leave.

6. Learn More – Even with the pressure and intensity of the season, a coach should not put learning on hold. A post-game or post-training session routine can be effective so the coaching staff can reflect on what works and what does not. In addition, a coach should always push their limits and try new experiences, even if there is a high risk of failure.

7. Question Everything – Part of becoming successful is challenging every traditional assumption about how we work. Traditional training programs are filled with irrelevant activities that waste vital time and energy. Sometimes, improving an environment is about subtraction rather than addition.

8. Find Feedback – Don't judge your coaching by results. Instead find ways to measure both the team and individual player's progress throughout the season. This can be invaluable when setbacks arise and also when you need to evaluate the season and be as specific as possible about growth.

9. Acknowledge Weaknesses and Find Help – No coach is perfect and knowing your areas of weakness does not make you weak. Do not cling to the belief that you can do everything your team requires and instead find staff who specialize in areas that you don't.

10. Enjoy it! – The life of a coach is not easy. You have to make difficult decisions that not everyone will agree with, you will face criticism when things go wrong, and you will feel unappreciated for most of the time. But the good always outweighs the bad so the journey should always be enjoyed!

Conclusion

Naturally, pre-season is a time for hope and excitement for coaches. It is also, however, a time to set standards, build relationships, create player buy-in, install effective communication systems, and, most importantly, to prepare one's team physically, tactically, mentally, and technically for the season ahead. Coaches today, therefore, have a massive responsibility to both their team and staff. It takes a lot of work and commitment to get things right, and it also requires a fair amount of help.

The growth of sports science and psychology in the game over the past ten years has changed the landscape and significantly raised the bar on performance. They have also put major question marks on the ability of the modern coach to adapt. You are no longer training a team, but instead you are preparing athletes and leading people. The era of telling players to run around and expecting them to improve is long gone.

Coaching today is about growing, moving outside of comfort zones, inspiring everyone around you, and going beyond perceived limits. The same things that we ask of our players, we must demand of ourselves. Pre-season is the time to start the journey and set the foundation. The better we become at starting this process, the better our chances of success when the final whistle blows in the last game. And who knows, maybe even one day, the players will start to look forward to it as much as the coaches do!

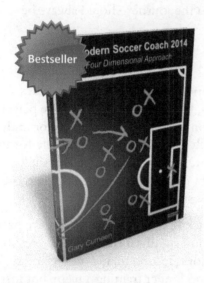

The Modern Soccer Coach 2014: A Four Dimensional Approach by Gary Curneen

Aimed at Soccer coaches of all levels and with players of all ages and abilities The Modern Soccer Coach 2014 identifies the areas that must be targeted by coaches who want to maximize a team's potential – the Technical, Tactical, Physical, and Mental sides to the game.

The Modern Soccer Coach 2014 offers contemporary focused and distilled insight into what soccer coaches need to do, and how! Filled with practical no-nonsense explanations, focused players drills and more than 30 illustrated soccer templates, The Modern Soccer Coach 2014 will help you – the modern coach - to create team performances that win match after match!

The Modern Soccer Coach: Position-Specific Training by Gary Curneen

In recent years, player development has been a hot topic in the soccer world. With more pressure on coaches to win than ever before, the modern game seems to be less about actual players and more about tactical systems. In many places, the majority of training sessions are structured so that each player receives the same training as his or her teammates, even though they are asked to perform different functions. As a result, players do not receive specific feedback and lack the ability to produce functional skills in the heat of a game.

Aimed at football coaches of all levels, and players of all ages and abilities, The Modern Soccer Coach: Position-Specific Training seeks to identify, develop, and enhance the skills and functions of the modern soccer player whatever their position and role on the pitch.

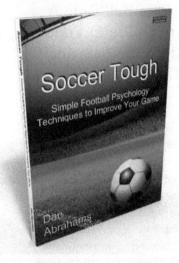

Soccer Tough: Simple Football Psychology Techniques to Improve Your Game by Dan Abrahams

"Take a minute to slip into the mind of one of the world's greatest soccer players and imagine a stadium around you. Picture a performance under the lights and mentally play the perfect game."

Technique, speed and tactical execution are crucial components of winning soccer, but it is mental toughness that marks out the very best players – the ability to play when pressure is highest, the opposition is strongest, and fear is greatest. Top players and coaches understand the importance of sport psychology in soccer but how do you actually train your mind to become the best player you can be? Soccer Tough demystifies this crucial side of the game and offers practical techniques that will enable soccer players of all abilities to actively develop focus, energy, and confidence. Soccer Tough will help banish the fear, mistakes, and mental limits that holds players back.

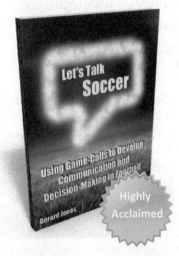

Let's Talk Soccer: Using Game-Calls to Develop Communication and Decision-Making in Football
by Gerard Jones

Let's Talk Soccer is a practical resource on how to develop communication in game-realistic practices that will increase creativity and skill across all ages. This book is based on tried and tested methods, offering you a framework using 'keywords' directly linked to your playing style. The book will help you develop a clear coaching language such that, when used in training and in games, your players will instantly understand what you mean and can consolidate their learning. Let's Talk Soccer is for professional and amateur soccer coaches across all levels of the game.

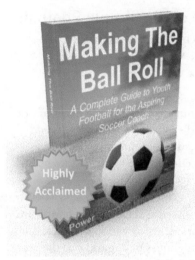

Making The Ball Roll: A Complete Guide to Youth Football for the Aspiring Soccer Coach by Ray Power

Making the Ball Roll is the highly acclaimed, complete guide to coaching youth soccer.

This focused and easy-to-understand book details training practices and tactics, and goes on to show you how to help young players achieve peak performance through tactical preparation, communication, psychology, and age-specific considerations. Each chapter covers, in detail, a separate aspect of coaching to give you, the football coach, a broad understanding of youth soccer development. Each topic is brought to life by the stories of real coaches working with real players. Never before has such a comprehensive guide to coaching soccer been found in the one place. If you are a new coach, or just trying to improve your work with players - and looking to invest in your future - this is a must-read book!

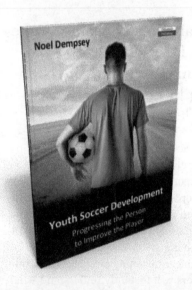

Youth Soccer Development: Progressing the Person to Improve the Player by Noel Dempsey

In "Youth Soccer Development", football coach Noel Dempsey examines where coaching has come from and where it is heading. Offering insights into how English football has developed, coaching methods, 'talent' in youngsters, and how a player's entire environment needs to be considered in coaching programmes - this book offers many touchpoints for coaches who want to advance their thinking and their coaching. Leaving specific onfield drills and exercises to other books, "Youth Soccer Development" digs deep into 'nature versus nature', players' core beliefs, confidence, motivation, and much more.

Developing the Modern Footballer through Futsal by
Michael Skubala and Seth Burkett

Aimed at coaches of all levels and ages, Developing the Modern Footballer through Futsal is a concise and practical book that provides an easy-to-understand and comprehensive guide to the ways in which futsal can be used as a development tool for football. From defending and attacking to transitional play and goalkeeping, this book provides something for everyone and aims to get you up-and-running fast.

Over 50 detailed sessions are provided, with each one related to specific football scenarios and detailing how performance in these scenarios can be improved through futsal. From gegenpressing to innovative creative play under pressure, this book outlines how futsal can be used to develop a wide range of football-specific skills, giving your players the edge.

The Footballer's Journey: real-world advice on becoming and remaining a professional footballer by Dean Caslake and Guy Branston

Many youngsters dream of becoming a professional footballer. But football is a highly competitive world where only a handful will succeed. Many aspiring soccer players don't know exactly what to expect, or what is required, to make the transition from the amateur world to the 'bright lights' in front of thousands of fans. The Footballer's Journey maps out the footballer's path with candid insight and no-nonsense advice. It examines the reality of becoming a footballer including the odds of 'making it', how academies really work, the importance of attitude and mindset, and even the value of having a backup plan if things don't quite work out.

Deliberate Soccer Practice: 50 Passing & Possession Football Exercises to Improve Decision-Making by Ray Power

Aimed at football coaches of all levels, but with a particular emphasis on coaches who work with youth players, *50 Passing & Possession Football Exercises to Improve Decision-Making* is comprised of 20 Technical Practices and 30 Possession Practices. They are carefully designed to be adaptable to suit the needs of the players you work with; to challenge them and give them decisions to make. The sessions look to make soccer complex and realistically difficult – no passing in queues from one cone to the next with no interference. Crucially, the exercises offer a means to accelerate player development effectively and enjoyably. Part of the *Deliberate Soccer Practice* series.

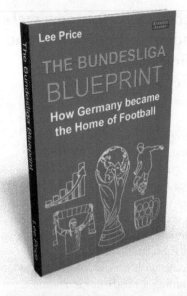

The Bundesliga Blueprint: How Germany became the Home of Football by Lee Price

In this entertaining, fascinating, and superbly-researched book, sportswriter Lee Price explores German football's 10-year plan. A plan that forced clubs to invest in youth, limit the number of foreign players in teams, build success without debt, and much more. The Bundesliga Blueprint details how German fans part-own and shape their clubs, how football is affordable, and the value of beer and a good sausage on match days. The book includes interviews from Michael Ballack, Jens Nowotny and Christoph Kramer, and the movers-and-shakers behind Germany's leading clubs including Schalke, Dortmund, and Paderborn.

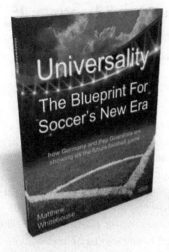

Universality | The Blueprint for Soccer's New Era: How Germany and Pep Guardiola are showing us the Future Football Game by Matthew Whitehouse

The game of soccer is constantly in flux; new ideas, philosophies and tactics mould the present and shape the future. In this book, Matthew Whitehouse – acclaimed author of The Way Forward: Solutions to England's Football Failings - looks in-depth at the past decade of the game, taking the reader on a journey into football's evolution. Examining the key changes that have occurred since the turn of the century, right up to the present, the book looks at the evolution of tactics, coaching, and position-specific play. They have led us to this moment: to the rise of universality. Universality | The Blueprint For Soccer's New Era is a voyage into football, as well as a lesson for coaches, players and fans who seek to know and anticipate where the game of the future is heading.

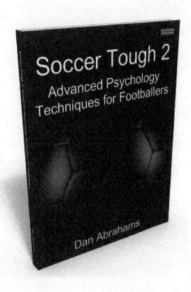

Soccer Tough 2: Advanced Psychology Techniques for Footballers by Dan Abrahams

In Soccer Tough 2: Advanced Psychology Techniques for Footballers Dan introduces soccer players to more cutting edge tools and techniques to help them develop the game of their dreams. Soccer Tough 2 is split into four sections – Practice, Prepare, Perform, and Progress and Dan's goal is simple – to help players train better, prepare more thoroughly, perform with greater consistency and progress faster.

Each section offers readers an assortment of development strategies and game philosophies that bring the psychology of soccer to life. They are techniques that have been proven on pitches and with players right across the world.

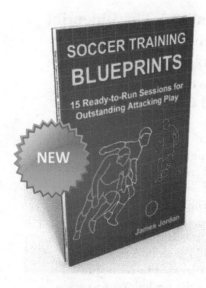

Soccer Training Blueprints: 15 Ready-to-Run Sessions for Outstanding Attacking Play by James Jordan

Are you a coach for whom time is tight? Would you like to get hands on with ready-to-use session templates, quickly? Then this book is for you! Utilising a game-based approach to soccer – where individuals actually play games rather than growing old in semi-static drills – author James Jordan offers 15 detailed session plans (comprised of 75 cutting-edge exercises) to help coaches develop attacking mindsets and improved skills in their players, and, most of all, nurture a love for soccer. Through his approach, James has won six High School State Championships and one Classic 1 Boys' Club Championship over the past decade. Aimed at coaches of both young male and female players, from 5-18 years of age, and adaptable depending on age group and skill set, each illustrated session plan is organized in an easy-to-understand format. This is the sister book to *The Volunteer Soccer Coach* (if you already have a copy of this book, do not purchase Soccer Training Blueprints).

A Special Book

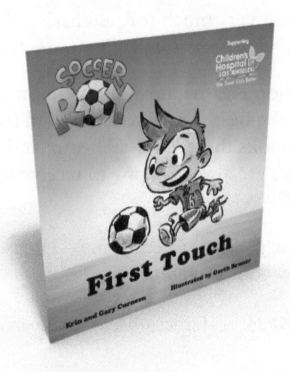

Soccer Roy: First Touch
by Erin Curneen, Gary Curneen, Garth Bruner

Please let me introduce you,
To a joyful baby boy,
With big blue eyes and a welcoming smile,
He goes by the name of Roy.

Gary and Erin Curneen wrote this children's book to forever honor their son Roy, who lived a brief life, and to give back to the hospital that gave them three weeks with their baby boy. Erin gave birth to Roy on December 3, 2014, and he was immediately taken into the care of Children's Hospital Los Angeles, due to a congenital diaphragmatic hernia. Even though Roy could not be saved, Gary and Erin were overwhelmed by the care that their son received and felt a strong urge to give back in some way. Their hope is that Roy's memory can forever make a difference in the lives of children. **All profits received from this book will be donated to Children's Hospital Los Angeles.**

Thank you very much for purchasing this copy of *The Modern Soccer Coach: Pre-Season Training*.

At Bennion Kearny, it is our intention to try to provide the best soccer coaching and football-related books that we possibly can, and for that matter we are always happy to receive readers' feedback.

So, please feel free to email me – James – and let me know your thoughts!

James   James@BennionKearny.com

Learn More about our Books at:

www.BennionKearny.com/Soccer

Printed in July 2019
by Rotomail Italia S.p.A., Vignate (MI) - Italy